Couples Connecting: Prerequisites of Intimacy

Couples Connecting: Prerequisites of Intimacy has been co-published simultaneously as *Journal of Couples Therapy*, Volume 9, Numbers 1/2 2000.

Couples Connecting: Prerequisites of Intimacy

Barbara Jo Brothers
Editor

Couples Connecting: Prerequisites of Intimacy has been co-published simultaneously as *Journal of Couples Therapy*, Volume 9, Numbers 1/2 2000.

Routledge
Taylor & Francis Group
New York London

Couples Connecting: Prerequisites of Intimacy has been co-published simultaneously as *Journal of Couples Therapy*, Volume 9, Numbers 1/2 2000.

First published by

The Haworth Press, Inc., 10 Alice Street, Binghamton, NY 13904-1580 USA

This edition published 2012 by Routledge

Routledge	Routledge
Taylor & Francis Group	Taylor & Francis Group
711 Third Avenue	27 Church Road
New York, NY 10017	Hove, East Sussex BN3 2FA

Cover design by Thomas J. Mayshock Jr.

Library of Congress Cataloging-in-Publication Data

Couples connecting: prerequisites of intimacy/Barbara Jo Brothers, editor.

p. cm.

Includes bibliographical references and index.

ISBN 0-7890-1164-6 (alk. paper: acid-free paper)–ISBN 0-7890-1165-4 (alk. paper: acid-free paper)

1. Marital psychotherapy. I. Brothers, Barbara Jo, 1940-

RC488.5 .C6434 2000
616.89′156–dc21

00-058133

Couples Connecting: Prerequisites of Intimacy

CONTENTS

ABOUT THE EDITOR

Barbara Jo Brothers, MSW, BCD, a Diplomate in Clinical Social Work, National Association of Social Workers, is in private practice in New Orleans. She received her BA from the University of Texas and her MSW from Tulane University, where she is currently on the faculty. She was Editor of *The Newsletter of the American Academy of Psychotherapists* from 1976 to 1985, and was Associate Editor of *Voices: The Art and Science of Psychotherapy* from 1979 to 1989. She has 30 years of experience, in both the public and private sectors, helping people to form skills that will enable them to connect emotionally. The author of numerous articles and book chapters on authenticity in human relating, she has advocated healthy, congruent communication that builds intimacy as opposed to destructive, incongruent communication which blocks intimacy. In addition to her many years of direct work with couples and families, Ms. Brothers has led numerous workshops on teaching communication in families and has also played an integral role in the development of training programs in family therapy for mental health workers throughout the Louisiana state mental health system. She is a board member of the Institute for International Connections, a non-profit organization for cross-cultural professional development focused on training and cross-cultural exchange with psychotherapists in Russia, republics once part of what used to be the Soviet Union, and other Eastern European countries.

Virginia Satir and Wholeness

Barbara Jo Brothers

Virginia Satir had a dream threading through her process communities, which had evolved from the month long seminars she began leading in 1969. The dream had various captions, which also evolved over time: Peoplemaking (Satir, 1977), The University for Becoming Human, The University for Becoming More Human, The University for Becoming More Fully Human (Satir, 1977, 1981, 1982, 1983).

Virginia's game was wholeness. Actually it was no game; it was a passion nestled in the core of her being. We had among us–we of the mental health field–a person who consciously and deliberately worked to shift human behavior across the planet.

The following excerpts trace the thread of that dream.

UNIVERSITY FOR BEING MORE FULLY HUMAN

From a letter written organizing Avanta, the Virginia Satir Network:

> I have a dream of developing what I am tentatively calling the University for Being More Human, which is an extension of the month-long training programs I have been doing for the past nine years. I see this as eventually becoming part of the whole Network family. Like all dreams, this one is subject to revision and review . . .
>
> (Satir, 1977)

[Haworth co-indexing entry note]: "Virginia Satir and Wholeness." Brothers, Barbara Jo. Co-published simultaneously in *Journal of Couples Therapy* (The Haworth Press, Inc.) Vol. 9, No. 1/2, 2000, pp. 1-4; and: *Couples Connecting: Prerequisites of Intimacy* (ed: Barbara Jo Brothers) The Haworth Press, Inc., 2000, pp. 1-4.

From Process Community Meeting II, August 1982:

> No maps . . . [when I saw my first family, in 1951], no maps. There are no maps for what we're doing here. We and you, you and us are making those maps as you go through the experience. So I am not thinking in terms of the finished product, because I think we haven't known very much in this world about how and how far we can go. Most of what we know about human beings we got from studying sick people. We don't know much about well people. We don't even know much about how human beings grow and develop. So we are at the beginning of something very exciting and important . . . .
>
> (Satir, 1982)

Process Community III, August 19, 1983:

> . . . the formation of something in my mind that I called "*The University for Being More Fully Human.*"
>
> Now I have had long and wide exposure with almost every professional, educational arm that there is: psychology, nursing, theology, psychiatry, medicine, the arts, management of all sorts of education in the universities. And I was often offered posts to come and stay three months and do this or that. Anyway, the point was that I began, in those earlier years to say to myself, What's lacking in the university is [the looking] for [and the teaching] what makes people *human.* I was aware that the instrument that we *are* is what makes us successful or not successful in using the knowledge that we have. None of that was touched and still isn't being touched in many of the university areas . . . if we really understand . . . everybody is unique. That means you cannot deal with [simply] looking [only] at sameness and differentness, you have to look at it in terms of the process. So everyone needs to be in touch with their uniqueness. There is no comparison in uniqueness. All right. So [now] I'm looking at a very different kind of group, evolving . . . by the way, I know that everyone can evolve. And I stretch my neck and my back and my interest and my love and all the rest [of me] in all my seminars to help each person to come to that flowering place. *Because I know when all of these lights are on that the whole world will be*

lighted in a different way. And I know it is possible, it just depends on how long it will take.

(Satir, 1983, p. 741)

Of course, Virginia Satir was not the first and only person interested in creating a "better" world. However, her unique stance had nothing to do with "good" versus "bad."

WHOLENESS RATHER THAN GOOD AND BAD

. . . I also know deep down that these [domestic atrocities] are outcomes of people whose coping mechanisms are such that this is what [it is about]. Fortunately . . . , I've done enough with people like that to know what's underneath. It had nothing to do with love or intention, it is about survival.

As an example, take a parent, a young woman 16 years old, or 17. Having a child before she's ready and her gonads are working so she's got some man around older than herself who is an alcoholic. And she wants very much to hang onto this man, the kid somehow needs her when she wants to do something else someplace else, her needs and the child's need collide. And at a certain point she settles for her needs but at the same time she feels guilty about it, the kid picks up on that and starts to nag. And the nagging crying gets to her and she wants some shut up so she can get those places out of her head, and slaps the child in such a way that can hurt the child even then. Then the child cries some more in the same way and that eats on her and pretty soon the child is either seriously hurt or dead.

It has nothing to do with love, and once we get that through our head, I think we will be a lot further ahead. It has to do with wholeness of ourselves. Whole people and people who love themselves do not behave that way. They don't have to.

So, that is why I don't really care much about "good or bad." I think they're both in the same category. What I do [care about and hope to facilitate] is "whole and real"–as much as I know about. When I can develop wholeness for people standing on their own feet, that they have their own radiation and they don't have to ask anybody else to [turn on] the lights.[1] So they don't have to be nagging people . . . But many of us are far away from

> that, some of the time, some of us a lot of the time, some of us haven't been there yet. (That doesn't mean anybody here [in this room], I know, because you couldn't be here unless you had that [capacity for autonomy].
>
> That's one of the reasons why professional education comes to people. I think it is essential, essential that we work with our own [bodied selves] before we ever try to fiddle around with anybody's life.
>
> (Satir, 1981, p. 121)

The following lecture, titled, "Hope, Wholeness, and Helping The Flat to Grow Round" (a transcription from Satir, 1981), was presented during a 30 day seminar which also included, other lectures, demonstrations and exercises. The seminars reflected the concept of wholeness in structure as well as in content. Virginia Satir understood the value of presenting her material on sensory, cognitive, and affective levels. For this reason, such lectures were always imbedded in a rich loam of experiential activity.

NOTES

1. In editing Virginia Satir's verbally delivered lectures for readable written text, there is a danger of over-simplifying her concepts–which are rich, complex, and a radical departure from "fix-the-symptom" modes of therapy.

Virginia is saying (1) she knows how to help people develop wholeness; (2) a person developing wholeness is a person becoming aware of their own radiance and inner resources; (3) such a person is, therefore, not dependent on others to "turn on the lights"; (4) this person would not be subject to the kind of desperation that engenders abusive behavior.

In other words, bring the person to full, respectful awareness of their own inner resources, and symptoms become irrelevant and vanish. She knew this worked because she was able to bring it about in patients.

REFERENCES

Satir, V. (1977, January). Draft. Letter to Sponsors. University for Being More Human. Santa Barbara, CA: Virginia Satir Archives, Special Collection. Davison Library. University of California.

Satir, V. (1981). First process community, Park City, Utah. Unpublished transcript.

Satir, V. (1982). Presentation at Avanta Process Community II, in Crested Butte, CO.

Satir, V. and Banmen, J. (1983). *Virginia Satir verbatim.* John Banmen Delta Psychological Associates, Inc. 11213 Canyon Crescent, North Delta, British Columbia, Canada V4E 2R6.

Hope, Wholeness, and Helping the Flat to Grow Round

Virginia Satir

ROUND AND NOT FLAT

. . . I believe that people were meant to be round not flat, and so I can no longer turn my back on the absolute assurance to myself that people were made to be round. True, we have been surrounded for thousands of years by things that have asked us to be flat. You would not be here unless you believed in round people. It is natural for sickness to be with flatness and health to be with roundness, if you follow my metaphor. So, when we come tomorrow, one of the things you will know is I will be doing everything I can to respect whatever flatness I find, because that is a place that many people begin–and go towards roundness.

Yesterday you probably became aware that my work in working with people would follow how I view things. I think there's a definite relationship between how someone sees something and how they proceed. This makes a foundation to my work of trying to help people be round: that means, to help people to be in touch with all their parts.

SYMPTOMATOLOGY

That also gives you the basis of my ideas about symptomatology. I believe that symptomatology is that which occurs because we are

---

[Haworth co-indexing entry note]: "Hope, Wholeness, and Helping the Flat to Grow Round." Satir, Virginia. Co-published simultaneously in *Journal of Couples Therapy* (The Haworth Press, Inc.) Vol. 9, No. 1/2, 2000, pp. 5-9; and: *Couples Connecting: Prerequisites of Intimacy* (ed: Barbara Jo Brothers) The Haworth Press, Inc., 2000, pp. 5-9.

unnourished and unconnected and inharmonious. And there are many cognitive ways to talk about that, so that if I am going to help somebody with whatever their symptoms are, I am going to go toward helping them to nurture themselves; to nurture themselves, and to get in touch with things that are present but they don't know about, to find access to the things that they have they haven't been able to access; then to help them make connections with themselves in the interest of themselves. And that is an over-simplified way of talking about how to go toward roundness–to move toward growth and wholeness.

HOW TO MAKE "ROUNDNESS" RATHER THAN HOW TO STAMP OUT SYMPTOMS

Now I'll just make one little comment here. Most of us–and I don't know how true this is: When I say "us," I'm talking about another "us." I don't always know you that well.Those who have any training in helping people often have become expert in mental *ill* health. And that means that the focus of where we have come from, most of us, has been looking at the ill health here, or the symptom. That becomes the center of what we do. Everything else fans out from this. So that what we do and what we've learned for the most part, has been how to take the ill-health aspect and try to do something with *that.*

I don't work that way any more (i.e., dealing with dis-ease), I used to. I work on the principle that here is a being that is not yet fully in touch with all the aspects of their health, the resources that they have. And the symptom shows up as a kind of blockage in that. So I start from how to develop health rather than to get rid of ill-health. To me, that is a very important difference. So to put it oversimplified, my goal is how to develop health rather than to get rid of ill-health. Now if I do this, develop health, then there is no need for ill-health. That is an orientation; you can say I am working here about how to make roundness instead of how to stamp something out.

I want to make one other comment about that . . . All the things I have learned about blisters, pain, difficulties, struggles, and all that, I still know, but I use it differently. So this is not an invitation to get rid of everything, no more than it is an invitation when we are an adult to forget all the learnings of our childhood. Because we keep moving and growing in terms of our experience.

Sometimes when I speak like this people say, "Oh, then all the things I learned about _____don't fit?" No, they fit, but they are used in a different way. Now we are hearing a lot about holistic health and holistic medicine, and what that means really is that we are adding to what we know and using our information differently. The word is "and," not "either/or."

I want to also say that at this point in time all over the world, there are people who have glimpses of what it would be like to be fully functioning people. So one of the challenges is how to take the information that we have and apply it in such a way that it promotes health rather than stamping out illness. So that is the way you will see me operate. Sometimes when people watch what I do in families, they say it is magic and only I can do it. Not true. It is because of the way that I use what I have. I will tell you a little story about that. In the early sixties, when I started working like this it was freaking everybody out. I was a nice freak but I was still a freak. And one of the things that happened very early in California through a whole series of funny things, is people wanted me to train them in family therapy, and so I followed the principle that I would show people. I wasn't going to talk about it, I would show. And I would work with people who had been in the hospital 18, 19, 20 years. Patients in state hospitals. Now at that time, everybody knew, once a chronic, always a chronic. And our hospitals were fully of decaying, vegetating people. I said, "I want to work with the population. I want to get somebody who has been in the hospital 18 or 19 years who still has a family. And I worked in every state hospital in California, and every one of those people got out of the hospital in 10 weeks, after having been there 18 or 20 years. And then people said, "You know, maybe we made a mistake in diagnosis." I said, "uh-uh. What you noticed led you to that conclusion. I look at different things so I come out in another way." That [series of events] was one of the big elements in starting the movement to change and get rid of those kinds of wards.

So the point of what I am making now is we can focus on anything, and the result of what we focus on is going to show up in what happens. So if I focus on that which is getting you to accent your resources, then you are going to grow. If I focus on that which is all your bad points and try to get rid of them, both of us are engaged in a killing operation. That is the way I see it today.

So how are we going to use the fact that you are too thin, that you are not eating? How are we going to use the fact that you don't see any meaning in life and you call that depression and maybe an invitation to suicide? How are we going to use the fact that at a moment in time you react in such a way that you are blind and deaf and you killed somebody? How are you going to react so that [same] energy can be used [,instead,] in a growth way? Those are some of the challenges that I have given myself and I have seen them pay off all over the world.

WHERE THERE IS LIFE, THERE IS HOPE

If you were to leave this seminar with the idea–you probably had it when you came in–that *human life and life itself is always capable of growth,* whether in a 94 year old, a two day old, or in 40 year old. If you come away with the idea that growth is always possible because we are dealing with life and life is capable, always, of growing, that is the nature of it, then you will never have burn-out again in your work, never–that I can tell you. You may have pain because the world is full of pain, but you will never have burn-out, because you will always know some place to go. Always have that. And I suppose that that is probably one of the reasons why, for me, I can go anywhere in the world to any kind ____, any kind of difficulty, and know that I can go somewhere, because, one, I am working with life, and two, always that possibility is there because there is life. And if you have that, then what to do is to get into a creative place with whomever you work.

And I don't know what that feels like when I tell you that. What does it feel like? It is not another should, it is not that you should, but it is possible. Do you ever have burn-out? The quickest road to burn-out is to figure out that you have got to solve problems and get rid of something–the shortest road to it, because none of us can do it really. I don't know how it is now, but it used to be the way you closed a case was that they either died, moved away or got too old.

So, I surround what I do with life, with hope, knowing absolutely that the human being has that possibility. It may not have been [known] at the time. And it may also be that you at this moment in time feel too afraid or hopeless or whatever to connect with that. There is nothing wrong or right with that, but [nevertheless hope] *is* always possible for the people you know.

(Satir, 1981, pp. 80-86)

REFERENCE

Satir, V. (1981). First process community, Park City, Utah. Unpublished transcript.

Developmental Prerequisites of Intimacy

Au-Deane Shepherd Cowley

SUMMARY. There are prerequisites that must be achieved developmentally before individuals are capable of co-creating healthy intimacy in adult relationships. Thus, therapists often have to work to help client systems overcome failures of maturation. In these kinds of therapeutic encounters the therapist acts as a developmental partner. By designing compensatory experiences, the therapist can help partners fill gaps in early development and education that operate to sabotage loving relationships. This paper offers examples of how levels of moral development and social-perspective taking can be utilized within a transpersonal approach to help couples achieve more satisfying intimate connections. *[Article copies available for a fee from The Haworth Document Delivery Service: 1-800-342-9678. E-mail address: <getinfo@haworthpressinc.com> Website: <http://www.HaworthPress.com>]*

KEYWORDS. Healthy intimacy, cultural context for intimacy, developmental prerequisites, ego strengths, developmental partnering, developmental deficits, structure building, moral development, social perspective taking, spiritual component, transpersonal approach

INTRODUCTION

According to Erich Fromm (1959) human beings have an imperative need to be related and united with other human beings. The

Au-Deane Shepherd Cowley, PhD, is Corresponding Author, Professor Emerita of Social Work, University of Utah, 1931 South Moor Drive, Salt Lake City, UT 84117.

[Haworth co-indexing entry note]: "Developmental Prerequisites of Intimacy." Cowley, Au-Deane Shepherd. Co-published simultaneously in *Journal of Couples Therapy* (The Haworth Press, Inc.) Vol. 9, No. 1/2, 2000, pp. 11-35; and: *Couples Connecting: Prerequisites of Intimacy* (ed: Barbara Jo Brothers) The Haworth Press, Inc., 2000, pp. 11-35. Single or multiple copies of this article are available for a fee from The Haworth Document Delivery Service [1-800-342-9678, 9:00 a.m. - 5:00 p.m. (EST). E-mail address: getinfo@haworthpressinc.com].

fulfillment of this basic need for a sense of belonging and connection is so fundamental that Fromm further posited that our very sanity depends on getting it met. Exploding rates for divorce, separation, single head of household, and dual career marriages all cause one to wonder about the discrepancy between the support and closeness required to keep our relationships and culture sane, and the social indicators that seem to demonstrate that human relationships are in more trouble in the nineties than perhaps ever before. As George Leonard once pointed out:

> We can orbit the earth, touch the moon, and yet this society has not devised a way (though love propels our very existence) for man and woman to live together for seven straight days with any assurance of harmony. (Wegscheider-Cruse, 1988, p. viii)

So, though the desire for interpersonal harmony is great, and the impulse toward self-fulfillment instinctive (Szent-Gyerogyi, 1974), achieving either one in the postmodern age is a rare phenomenon. Could it be that the cultural milieu in which we are embedded is not hospitable to the moral maturation demanded for healthy intimacy within relationships?

THE CULTURAL CONTEXT

Miller (1995) opined that "no interpretation of intimacy that ignores its social setting can possibly be adequate" (p. 9). What kind of preparation for intimacy do the young receive in America today? According to Miller:

> We live in a culture that still believes in a kind of frontier ideology, which promotes competitive self-realization rather than cooperative, empathic balance between self and other. (Miller, 1995, p. 108)

Not only are youth encouraged to be separate rather than connected, they are also surrounded with media advertising and sitcom inanities that portray exploitive ways of relating to the opposite sex. Far from being funny, the result of a steady diet of soap opera versions of life is taking a terrible psychological toll:

> We have become so thoroughly disillusioned with love that we are on the verge of becoming a culture of cynics about one of our

> most cherished traditional values–the ideal of romantic love. (Miller, 1995, p. 11)

The institution of the family is not faring any better in terms of the modeling that is presented on television and in other media. When the primacy of the marital relationship is undervalued the quality of family life suffers:

> We have, as a culture, overloaded the institution of marriage with so many expectations that it crumbles beneath the psychological burden. The family is increasingly a beleaguered phenomenon, shunted to the sidelines of cultural interest. Similarly, friendship is becoming an activity that people wish they had time for. Yet we grow only with and through others. Devaluation of relatedness is another form of destroying our environment: we trample on that which constitutes our world. (Josselson, 1996, p. 13)

Most therapists would agree with Nathaniel Branden's (1982) assertion that "marriage is not for children." However, in a culture plagued with immaturity of all kinds, there are few people that exhibit other than child-like behaviors. Lamentably, the cultural context in America in the nineties is one that leaves authors and social commentators asking questions like: "Whatever happened to adulthood?" (Simon, 1996). Dumb and dumber has not only been accepted as entertaining, but it is also a common practice to showcase stars who model that it isn't "in" to have values or to be respectful of intimate others. Referring to Robert Bly (1996), Simon (1996) points out that the paucity of admiration and the dismissal of anything that smacks of lofty aspiration "may be the most troubling sign of our cultural decay" (p. 55):

> At least, that is the thesis of *The Sibling Society,* Bly's latest book–a look at the epidemic of self-absorption and spiritual sterility he sees sweeping through America today. The root of our malaise, says Bly, is that we've become a nation of people who refuse to grow up and are neglecting the most important task of adulthood: preparing the next generation to take its place in the world. (Simon, 1996, pp. 55-56)

Finding ways to mentor the next generation toward adulthood presents a challenge to those who use an interpersonal approach in relationship therapy (Gurman, 1981). This is because even though therapists have generally done a good job of teaching communication skills requisite to healthy relationships and helping partners to have more insight into the early childhood issues that have impacted their adult relationships, other key factors related to developmental maturation may not have been emphasized. This paper posits that many partly or completely unsuccessful efforts by professionals to tip the balance in favor of healthy relationships may have been doomed because:

1. Therapists haven't always articulated clearly enough (for themselves or their client-systems) that there are developmental prerequisites that must be achieved by both partners before intimacy even becomes a possibility;
2. Therapists have not always explicitly taken on the task of being a developmental partner for each of the individuals in a couple system; and
3. Therapists have rarely accessed theories that offer generous enough expectations about human potential to provide the lure for becoming more fully human.

What happens to intimacy when "both our culture and our psychology deny our essential dependence upon each other" and the "yearning for responsiveness and contact that warms and enriches life" (Josselson, 1996, pp. 12-13) is not valued and therefore, seldom expressed? Can a person learn to be intimate in adulthood, if he/she never experienced or witnessed it as a child growing up? Is anyone able to single-handedly create and sustain a capacity for intimacy in a relationship if his/her partner devalues connection and makes distancing an art?

DEVELOPMENTAL PREREQUISITES

Throughout the evolution of psychological theory, many different voices have offered insights into the various kinds of developmental deficits that undermine an individual's dual desire for achieving self-fulfillment and interpersonal harmony. Yet, there still seems to be a general reticence among practitioners about specifically communicating to the clients they serve about the key role that developmental issues play in human relationships. Unlike the work of Father Freud who stated that the real work of psychotherapy was "soul making" (Bettelheim, 1983), or the transpersonal theory of Ken Wilber (Wilber, 1986) that openly promotes the goal of transforming consciousness, marital and family therapists have generally skirted around the importance of the process of psychological maturation. Some literature in the field has gently hinted about how the everyday give and take of a committed relationship may operate as a "forced" venue for helping people to become more psychologically mature. For example:

> Psychiatrist Robert Seidenberg maintains that marriage can provide the couple a means to hasten what he calls the "humanizing" process by providing opportunities for accommodation, for individuation, for the exchange of ideals and values, for the delineation of boundaries, for the testing of moralities and the mastery of erring instincts. (Wegscheider-Cruse, 1988, p. 30)

However, it would seem obvious that counting on a spontaneous humanizing process to occur in relationships that automatically causes couples to mature is not a viable alternative for the therapist concerned with individual maturation/happiness or family remediation/empowerment. While it's possible that marriage and committed relationships may provide the context in which a maturation process can occur, too often they become a battleground for negativity instead. Goldbart and Wallen (1994) have chillingly described how immature two-year-old egos too often play out the "unconscious tendency for partners to enlist one another in a re-creation of the past" (p. 25). Miller described the plight of such couples who get caught up in the battles of "intimate terrorism" as follows:

> Married couples walk into a therapist's consulting room . . . to place their relationship with all its culturally sanctified meanings, vanished passion, complicated loyalties, discarded dreams, and private suffering on an examining table . . . They often wind up in therapy because they have been living together in pain, able neither to get closer nor to separate. (Miller, 1995, pp. 25-26)

How can therapists help intimate partners to overcome such destructive impasses?

In Horney's classic work (1937) she stated that in relating to others individuals characteristically move in three directions: away from, against, or toward. Two of these three directions doom relationships to pain and loneliness because flight (moving away from, distancing or stonewalling) or fight (moving against the other in oppositional or adversarial ways) only serve to make problems worse instead of better. The challenge for the therapist is to help couples to move *toward* each other. Only when affilative and cooperative attitudes of good will become the dominant mode of relating do couples begin to walk a path with a heart. What must occur developmentally before individuals can identify and master more mature, productive and nurturing styles of relating?

ACCRUING EGO STRENGTHS REQUISITE FOR HEALTHY RELATING

In 1950 Erik Erikson developed a psychosocial theory that he called "The Eight Stages of Man." This developmental theory though clothed in the unconscious sexism of its time, offers understanding about the destructive impact that incomplete or faulty development can have on intimate relationships. Conversely, by pinpointing the key developmental tasks of each age and stage, Erikson's theory also identifies some of the ego strengths required for individual maturation and healthy relating. At each stage when the ascendant developmental task is not balanced in a positive direction, the individual's life takes an unhealthy turn. If developmental deficits and regressive tendencies prevail, the potential for experiencing pathology or problems in living is greatly enhanced. How the developmental tasks of each of the eight stages are balanced will determine whether or not the growing individual will develop the ego strengths required for intimacy in adult relationships. Erikson's eight states are:

1. *Stage one* occurs in infancy (1-18 months) and involves the need to balance trust versus mistrust to accrue the ego strength of hope. If this important first stage remains unbalanced, the individual may develop a core pathology that manifests as withdrawal. Withdrawing by any of its names, i.e., hiding, stonewalling, avoidance, and so forth, is the antithesis of intimacy. Without a sense of trust between two people, the experience of intimacy is unlikely.
2. *Stage two* occurs during early childhood (18 months to 4 years). The toddler must balance autonomy versus shame and self-doubt

to accrue the ego strength of will. A person with a disabled will may suffer from compulsion. Deficits at this stage of development show up later in intimate relationships as low self-esteem and shame-based behaviors that deeply undermine the development of intimacy.

3. *Stage three* encompasses the years of early school and play (4 to 6 years). During this stage it is critically important for the child to balance initiative versus guilt. If one does not master the ability to take initiative and make decisions, there is the risk of becoming crippled by inhibition and a passive attitude that breeds hostility. If this stage is balanced toward progression the ego strength of purpose is added to character structure. If a sense of guilt and inhibition predominate sexual intimacy is likely to be sabotaged.
4. *Stage four* (from 7-12) presents the developmental task of balancing the risks and opportunities of middle school age. A sense of industry must be balanced to overcome inferiority. If this does not occur the growing child is unable to overcome inertia and accrue the ego strength of competence. Without a solid sense of one's own worth, defensive communication and behaviors often proliferate to destroy the possibility of intimate understanding and connection. Rarely does anyone have the perfect (or even "good enough") childhood in terms of balancing all of the early developmental tasks. However, if one has accrued a relative sense of hope, will, purpose, and competence during early childhood, he/she is better prepared to face the challenging passage into adolescence.
5. *Stage five* occurs between the ages of 12-22. The imperative task for teens and young adults is to develop a strong sense of identity in order to avoid the pitfalls of identity diffusion and/or role confusion. Only when a sense of separate selfhood is achieved is an individual capable of exhibiting fidelity. If a person lacks a clear sense of what he/she believes and values, the suggestions and directives of others may be overwhelming. A person cannot be trusted if external voices determine behavior. Whenever a person feels unable to take a stand according to his/her own internal belief system and values, negative feelings of self-repudiation are likely to develop. In terms of relationships, not having a "self" to share can leave one feeling inadequate and developmentally

unable to connect at intimate levels. Without a secure sense of identity, one is likely to become resentful and critical of anyone else's self-definition.

6. *Stage six* presents developmental tasks appropriate for early adulthood (22-34). It calls for the individual to balance dual pulls between intimacy and isolation. This stage is exemplified by the conflicting urge to be independent while at the same time yearning to be in a close relationship with an intimate another. Mature love is the virtue or ego strength that is accrued when this stage is balanced. It requires that the growing person learn how to balance the imperatives of both the "seeker self" and the "merger self" (Sheehy, 1976). Since identity must precede intimacy, the successful reconciliation of the two currents of development at this stage is dependent upon how well individuals were able to develop an independent sense of self at stage five. Without the ego strength of fidelity and a capacity for mature love a committed relationship that lasts over time cannot be co-created or maintained (Erikson, Erikson, & Kivnick, 1986).
7. *Stage seven* (34-60) involves the mid-life task of balancing generativity versus self-absorption. Only when a person has the capacity to care about the needs of others as much as his/her own needs is that person able to be a nurturing parent or intimate partner. Without the ego strength of generative caring, the individual may be defined by a sense of rejectivity that is totally self-centered. If self-absorption is dominant one's preoccupation with self, and the fear of not getting one's needs met, becomes a barrier to love. True intimacy demands nothing less than the death of ego. Those who fail to sufficiently mature beyond self-absorption will experience only love's unhealthy pseudo substitutes like fusion, co-dependence, and possessiveness.
8. *Stage eight* is a moment of truth time that lasts from about age 60 until death. In the winter of one's life the debits and credits are tallied. As one seeks to remain vitally involved in life, one is only able to avoid a sense of stagnation and despair if enough ego strengths have been accrued over the life cycle to add up to a sense of wisdom. When life's developmental tasks have been balanced in a positive direction the spiral of development is balanced toward health. Then individuals and intimate partners are able to leave behind a legacy of trust and love for the next gener-

> ation. If too many of life's challenges have not been mastered, individuals may be overwhelmed in old age with a sense of disdain for self, others and life itself. This can start the next generation off with the belief that the universe is not a friendly place, and the resultant sense of mistrust that accompanies negative early experiences is thus set in motion.

At any age in the life cycle, if unresolved developmental tasks are revisited and balanced toward growth, the person can expand self-awareness and add ego strengths to character structure.

MOVING BEYOND CHILDHOOD CONSCIOUSNESS

Paradoxically, after years of striving to build a strong ego structure one is confronted as an adult with the reality that nothing less than a kind of ego death is required if one is to live in a state of relative peace or normative compatibility with self or others. This ability to move beyond what Allport (1959) called affective and cognitive provincialism develops out of a life-long process of decentration across the life span. It is approximated only as individuals evolve out of infantile, childish, and adolescent immaturities to move toward more evolved ways of feeling, thinking, and relating or what Gould (1978) has called "adult consciousness."

Allport (1959) opined that neuroses were best defined as stubborn self-centeredness. He wrote that the only way a therapist can be helpful is by helping the client achieve a value system and outlook that is more mature and more adult. Although it seems obvious that the help and hope for absorbing reactive behaviors, irrational ideas, illegitimate demands, and neurotic interactions does lie in helping individuals to grow up, it is easier said than done. Such growth requires the client to give up habit patterns of a lifetime that have become integral pieces of self-definition. It's no wonder that the invitation to change evokes resistance, yet change we must if we are to grow beyond our childish ways.

Developing an adult consciousness is only one aspect of the life-long process of becoming "the possible human" (Houston, 1982). Mature relating also requires that we learn how to take someone else's reality into account by communicating validating and empathic responses. Being an adult demands that we are able to put jointly negotiated priorities above personal pride. This is the kind of maturity that Steiner (1981) labeled "the other side of power." Chopra (1997) also has written about the importance of getting out of stubborn self-centeredness and moving beyond the kind of cultural scripting that favors egotistical goals.

> Most people are raised to pursue ego goals, often without question. The choice to remain on this level is always open, but you also have the choice to move onto the plane of spirit, with its very different goals. (Chopra, 1997, p. 157)

If one chooses to shift from the goal of self-protection to the plane of spiritual maturity he/she must learn to practice the art of "surrendering" ego for the sake of the relationship.

DEVELOPMENTAL THEORY AS A FOUNDATION FOR PRACTICE

Many a "brilliant" therapeutic intervention at the system level has been sabotaged by the immaturity of one member of the couple or family system. Nichols acknowledged this frustrating fact by pointing out, "No jolt to the system will resolve a person's narcissistic vulnerability, unresolved conflict, or psychopathology" (Nichols, 1987, p. xiv). Understanding how each individual's level of maturity impacts the functioning of the whole makes it easy to see why it is no longer considered taboo for marital and family therapists to assess individual dynamics as well as the functional level of the total system. As Nichols has observed:

> Clinicians need not be limited either to an individual or to a systems viewpoint, but can use both–just as a photographer may use telescopic as well as wide-angle lenses. (Nichols, 1984, p. 132)

In addition to urging a dual focus that assesses the developmental level of both the individual and the system, Nichols (1987) has also sought to put individual development at the center of marital and family work. If couples and families are ever to achieve transformative levels of physical-psycho-social-spiritual health, practitioners will need to employ potentializing interventions designed to help individuals evolve out of the unconscious, self-defeating immaturities of childhood (Bentz, 1989).

According to Bowen (1976) reaching high levels of self-differentiation and maturity is rarely achieved in therapy or out. Maturity is definitely not a gift of the gods or a matter of luck. Becoming whole by actualizing the mature potential of one's physical, emotional, cognitive, social, moral and spiritual dimensions is a hard-won battle of human growth and development (Cowley, 1996). It takes one on an evolutionary journey away from primary narcissism and toward a separate sense of self. Actualizing a self is a developmental precursor that opens up a possibility for transcending the little self and moving toward an expanded sense of Self capable of going "beyond ego" toward self-transcendence (Walsh & Vaughn, 1980).

DEVELOPMENTAL PARTNERING

One effective strategy for transcending immature egos is the utilization of "a corrective developmental experience with a therapist as a developmental organizer" (Krueger, 1989, p. 155). Like Maslow (1959), Kernberg (1980), Kegan (1982), Pine (1985), Basch (1988), and Krueger (1989) have emphasized the importance of understanding developmental theories in order to make deeper and more long-lasting interventions. For example, by conceptualizing which of Erikson's eight developmental tasks seem unbalanced in a given client-system, the therapist can design corrective experiences to remedy developmental lags, immaturities, or skill deficits. Wilber (1986) calls this process "structure building."

The constructivist-developmental paradigm also emphasizes the importance of education and skill building. It proposes that interpersonal competence depends upon the integration of a wide range of developmental experiences in various dimensions of being:

> As individuals move through stages of development, their strategies of reasoning across physical, social, and moral domains are transformed and become increasingly more efficient. (Rosen, 1988, p. 319)

When deficits of development produce ineffective adults, there is always hope that individuals can correct earlier unbalances and rise to more mature levels of functioning. However, wanting to revise old habit patterns and being able to do so are very different things. Maslow cautioned that therapeutic support was often necessary to sustain the individual's innate thrust toward maturation and self-realization:

> The impulses toward self-fulfillment, though instinctive, are very weak, so that, in contrast with all other animals who have strong instincts, these directional tendencies are very easily drowned out by habit, by wrong cultural attitudes toward them, by traumatic episodes, by erroneous education (Maslow, 1959, p. 133). . . . If we wish to help humans to become more fully human, we must realize not only that they try to realize themselves but also that they are reluctant or afraid to do so. Only by appreciating this dialectic between sickness and health can we hope to provide the compensatory experiences required to help tip the balance in favor of health. (Maslow, 1959, p. 135)

If the current trend toward the replacement of the culture of romance by the culture of abuse (Miller, 1995) is to be averted, it seems clear that humans must find more effective methods for helping each other to grow up. Where can therapists find assumptions and theoretic bases that will provide them with tools to help tip the delicate balance in intimate relationships in favor of maturity and health?

TOWARD A TRANSPERSONAL APPROACH

Some observers of our day believe we live in a culture of narcissism (Lasch, 1987). This makes the challenge of learning and teaching how to transcend self-interest even more imperative if nurturing relationships and secure holding environments are to be co-created in the homes of the couples and families who are seeking professional help. Since the epitome of human development for western psychologies and family therapy approaches has been to reach self-actualization, traditional theories have often failed to provide the expanded view of human potential required to inspire individuals and families toward states of maturation that go beyond ego. It may be that in our willingness to be satisfied with reaching a goal of "normal" functioning, or even to settle for an absence of pathology, we have sold ourselves and our client systems short.

Jung once observed that being normal was a splendid ideal for the unsuccessful, but for people who have far more ability than the average-restriction to the normal would signify the bed of Procrustes–unbearable boredom, infernal sterility and hopelessness (Jung, 1933). Today many normal human beings are not only feeling hopeless but are also suffering from an existential and spiritual angst some have referred to as "futurelessness" (Lifton, 1982). Trapped in a bed of mediocrity and materialism, yet somehow sensing the greatness that might be, one desperate (but often unverbalized) question goes begging for an answer: "Is this all there is?"

> There are too few healthy models in the media or in our society to which we can point. In the name of modernity we are creating dysfunctional societies that are breeding pathological behavior–violence, extreme competitiveness, suicide, drug abuse, greed, and environmental degradation–at every hand. Such behavior is an inevitable consequence when a society fails to meet the needs of its members for social bonding, trust, affection, and a shared sacred meaning. (Korten, 1995, p. 4)

Much that masquerades as depression in our secular and banalized culture might more accurately be described as spiritual malaise (Goldberg, 1980) or dis-spiritation (Jourard, 1971; Bugental & Bugental, 1984). Many of the couples and families who go to therapy appear to be locked in a kind of despair that may only find relief through the process of becoming more fully human. As Jung once sagely observed, the greatest and most important problems of life are all in a certain way insoluble. They can never be solved, but only outgrown.

In searching for a theoretical approach that can offer a more generous view of individual, couple, and family potential, practitioners working with couples and families are beginning to explore the comprehensive and inclusive perspective of transpersonal psychology (Weinhold, 1989; Cowley, 1999). For centuries Eastern traditions have contained what Western psychologies have lacked–guidelines for accessing the highest possibilities of human growth and potential (Cowley, 1993; Cowley & Derezotes, 1994; Kramer, 1995). By synthesizing the best of East and West, transpersonal psychology offers an enlarged view of human potential that "spans the full spectrum of human growth from infancy to enlightenment" (Walsh & Vaughn, 1996, p. 63). Transpersonal theory expands the spectrum of consciousness to include higher states of consciousness as "normal" and optimally healthy ways of being. Wilber's three general levels of consciousness include (Wilber, 1986):

1. *Prepersonal Level:* This level includes chaotic it (id), psychoses, narcissistic or borderline disorders, and other irrational or undifferentiated states.
2. *Personal Level:* The personal level of development includes individuated states capable of rational self-definition, and ranges from immature to self-actualized levels.
3. *Transpersonal Level:* This domain of development represents the farther reaches of human nature (Maslow, 1971). It includes levels of consciousness that are trans-rational because they go "beyond" the bounds of reason toward Self-transcendence.

Walsh and Vaughn, who are pioneers in transpersonal psychology, have described Wilber's spectrum of consciousness and inclusive transpersonal theory this way:

> He {Wilber} suggests that a consciousness displays a spectrum of levels and states with corresponding unconscious structures. He contends that different schools of psychology address different levels of this spectrum. The different schools are not contradictory and antagonistic, therefore, but complementary perspectives, each partially true. This spectrum view of consciousness forms the infrastructure for Wilber's ontological, epistemological, developmental, and evolutionary theories. (Walsh & Vaughn, 1996, p. 63)

By including moral and spiritual dimensions, Wilber's Full Spectrum of Consciousness Model (Wilber, 1986), provides a more accurate and integral conceptualization of individual functioning. It also offers new diagnostic categories to replace medical nomenclatures that have often failed to provide a good fit for family therapists. Posed between the thesis of modern science and the antithesis of constructivism, transpersonal theory provides a synthesis that honors both the empirical and the intuitive. Most importantly, it is a theory of human potential that provides technologies for helping client-systems reach the levels of moral and spiritual maturity required for intimate relating (Cowley, 1996; Cowley, 1999).

A DEVELOPMENTAL SCALE FOR ASSISTING MORAL DEVELOPMENT

A scale that may be helpful in assessing the moral maturation of individual members of a couple-system is the Kohlberg/Woolf Scale (Woolf, 1984) (see Table 1). Based on Kohlberg's (1981) research on moral development and modified by Woolf, this scale depicts six levels of moral development. With an ascending or upward spiral of development as well as a downward spiral that indicates an inversion or regressive trend, the scale presents a visual representation illustrating both healthy and malignant aspects of moral development. Helping clients get in touch with the dialectic pressure of the two currents that pull on us isometrically from birth to death (Wickes, 1966) is a critically important part of providing compensatory experiences. By acknowledging that humans beings are really "human becomings" (Bentz, 1989) who are constantly being pulled in opposing directions, the therapist can normalize the ambivalence that accompanies each exploratory shift toward a more capable and expanded way of "being-in-the-world" (Heidegger, 1962). Explicit recognition and discussion about regressive (sick) and progressive (healthy) trends of development help clients to understand the difficulty and frustration involved in the processes of unlearning and letting go that occurs as each successive developmental shift toward higher levels of differentiation takes place.

> Stage development follows an invariant sequence. A stage is never skipped and its order of appearance is never reversed. The process of development is one of differentiation and integration, with each successive stage comprising a hierarchical reorganization of old and new cognitive structures. Each newly emerging stage constitutes a transformation from the old way of knowing and provides the individual with a qualitatively different and more adequate way of knowing. An advance in stage offers the person wider perspectives, greater problem-solving effectiveness across a greater range of domains, and liberation from constraints of the former stage. (Rosen, 1988, p. 318)

By helping individuals to develop more mature ways of being in the world, the therapist is able to increase the possibility for more effective and inclusive relationships.

TABLE 1. Six Levels of Moral Development
Kohlberg, Woolf*

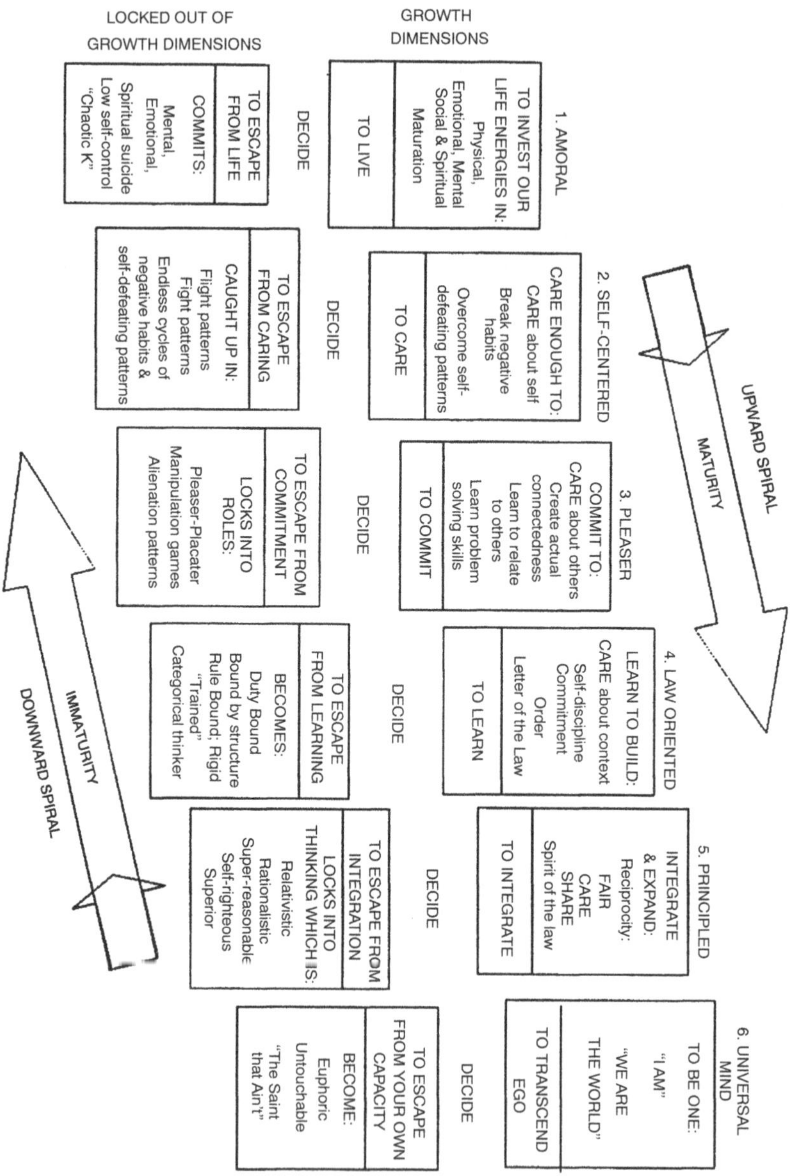

*Woolf, V. Vernon, PhD (1984). The Good Life Seminar. Provo, Utah.

CASE EXAMPLE

One couple presented classic issues demonstrating not only the developmental discrepancies that existed between the two of them, but also specific problems in terms of moral development and social role taking. Their frustrations were expressed in the kind of "different voices" that are internalized along with heterosexual "sex-roles" (Gilligan, 1982). In textbook fashion the male partner emphasized individual achievement over attachment, and the female partner defined herself within the context of a caring relationship (Viorst, 1986, p. 120).

The woman said one of the current problems she was experiencing was in trying to find a fair way to share the heavy work and responsibilities associated with remodeling and caring for their newly acquired home. Her statements were typically sprinkled with phrases like: "I don't like to nag. I would prefer to identify ways we could work together that would be fair for both of us. I am more than willing to share the work around the house, but I get frustrated when my husband is unwilling to even discuss what he believes his fair share of the work ought to be." The man's statements had an entirely different flavor to them. He tended to focus on defending his ego, and his personal discomfort at being put on the spot by saying things like: "I don't see why she is always finding fault with me, or wanting something more from me than I want to give. Why can't she just worship me and take care of me the way she did when we first got together?"

It doesn't take long for an objective third party to begin to pick up on the differences in level of moral development within such a couple-system. The more the wife communicated, the more she demonstrated a mature and principled level of moral development (Level 5 on the Kohlberg/Woolf Scale). The bulk of the husband's comments, however, fit neatly within the self-centered level (Level 2 on Kohlberg/Woolf Scale). The wife became even more frustrated when her husband continued to avoid the topic within the session, and seemed unable to discuss any problem without personalizing. It looked to me like the husband was so invested in focusing on how everything affected him (self-absorbed) that he had no energy left over to consider his wife's point of view or the relationship issues at stake.

By combining developmental theory from Erikson, Kohlberg/Woolf and Selman's Social Perspective-Taking (1971), it was possible to design interventions to help the husband develop an increased capacity for seeing things from another person's point of view. The husband, who was chronologically in his mid-forties, was functioning at an undifferentiated and egocentric level anticipated for children 3 to 6 years old or Level 0 according to Selman's Social Perspective-Taking Scale. The wife on the other hand was operating at Level 4 on Selman's Scale (Rosen, 1988, p. 328) (see Table 2).

If one member of a relationship system is unable to operate on at least Level 1, it will drag the relationship to Level 0 where intimacy cannot occur. By utilizing the scales of Kohlberg/Woolf or Selman, the therapist can sometimes objectify relationship issues and help both partners to reach the minimum prerequisite levels for intimacy, i.e., Level Five on the Kohlbeg/Woolf Scale and Level One on Selman.

To illustrate how to approach this kind of structure building, my first goal with the husband was focused on getting him involved in the

TABLE 2. Selman's Social Perspective-Taking Levels

0. Undifferentiated and egocentric (3-6 years)	Children resort to physical remedies to resolve personal problems. They confuse their own perceptions with the perceptions of others.
1. Differentiated and subjective (5-9 years)	Children make a clear differentiation between the perspectives of themselves and others. They realize that other people may feel differently in a given situation. They also realize that the same behavior in two different people may arise from different motives.
2. Self-reflective and reciprocal (7-12 yrs.)	Children can view themselves through another's eyes and can recognize that others have the same capability. This enables them to take into account another person's intentions.
3. Third-person and mutual (10-15 yrs.)	Children can assume the perspective of a hypothetical observer who coordinates the perspective of both the children and the persons they are interacting with. They also realize that others can do the same.
4. Social and conventional system (15 yrs. & above)	Adolescents have the ability to assume the viewpoint of an abstract-generalized other. They transcend their immediate environment to adopt a societal or national perspective, which embodies conventional, moral, and legal codes.

therapeutic process. I did this by saying something like: "You may be feeling your wife is putting you down when she talks about doing something more fair in relation to family chores. I believe she is only trying to get the two of you to think together about what might work best for *both* of you." By appealing to the husband's total absorption in self-interest I initially sought to build rapport and ameliorate resistance. Over time, one of my goals was to use my consistent modeling to help him move beyond his self-centered style and develop an increased capacity to see things from his wife's point of view. Only by cultivating an expanded awareness can he move "up" to a more mature level on Selman's Scale.

In working with the wife, structure building was not required. Instead, I sought to help her find ways to tolerate the frustration of living with an immature partner. It seemed helpful when I said to the wife, "I doubt your husband deliberately tries to avoid the issues that are important to you. It seems likely to me that he gets feeling so caught up in processing what the changes you are proposing may mean to him personally, that he is unable to focus on how the situation looks to you. In fact, when I hear you describe how spoiled he was as an only child, I can't help but wonder if he was ever taught how to consider how things looked to others as he was growing up."

Providing this kind of reframing feedback not only offers an empathic reply as verbal proof of my understanding of the wife's position, but also, at the same time, hopefully, generates some insight for her into her husband's behaviors. It is more helpful to the therapeutic process for partners to experience their mate as inept (due to developmental deficits) rather than as intentionally insensitive or "mean."

ANOTHER USE OF THE KOHLBERG/WOOLF SCALE

The six levels of moral development depicted in Table 1 can also be used to help couples understand how intimacy manifests across six different levels of development:

1. Level One: At the amoral level there is no motivation for intimacy. Interactions on level one are characterized by an "I don't care" attitude that precludes mutuality. Most couples experience non-caring times like this on occasion, but when this way of relating becomes a dominant pattern, it usually locks partners into a "shut down" mode which keeps them developmentally incapable of making a commitment to self, others, or the social context.

2. *Level Two:* At the self-centered level, communication is a duologue. Both partners do a lot of self-listening and pay little, if any attention to what the other is saying. Since self-interest reigns, neither person cares what the other thinks or feels. The total preoccupation of each partner with his/her own needs makes it impossible for either to validate or nurture the other. When even one partner operates at level two (or below) the depth of mutual caring required to co-create intimacy is not accessed.

3. *Level Three:* At level three, one or both of the individuals may be a "pleaser". If a person routinely pretends to be "as you want me to be," he/she usually becomes incapable of knowing or expressing authentic feelings. Since intimacy depends on an ability to share thoughts and feelings, fears and fantasies, hopes and dreams, it cannot grow in an emotional vacuum. Sometimes a partner will express the disappointment of trying to relate to a nonentity who never seems to have a new idea. Relating to a pleaser is like looking in a mirror to see only one's own reflection–or to experience the loneliness of hearing nothing but the echo of one's own voice.

4. *Level Four:* At the law-oriented level, relationships are rule-bound, closed, and rigid. Things are done by the book. Whenever the "letter of the law" mentality dictates, there is little leeway for spontaneity, novelty or surprise. When we are only allowed to be as we *should* be with one another, many elaborate rules and games have to be developed and routine reigns. Restrictive injunctions forbid healthy growth and change and leave little to no leeway for joy or healthy intimacy. Just as Kohlberg's research found that there are no solutions to problems when people operate morally on levels one through four, couples who function on those levels will not experience true intimacy. They may isolate, frustrate, accommodate, or dictate–but they will never really "relate" to each other as intimates.

5. *Level Five:* At level five true intimacy becomes a possibility. It is most likely to be achieved in a relationship wherein each partner is morally developed enough to operate out of principles like "fair," "care," and "share" (Woolf, 1984). Until both partners have accrued the mature capacities required for exhibiting principles such as unconditional love, reciprocity, empathy, generativity, and nurturing it is unlikely that these ego strengths will become the dominant mode in the relationship.

6. *Level Six:* Occasionally couples reach levels of moral maturity that

allow their relationship to express a transcendent love of All through attitudes of compassion, inclusiveness and charitable giving. Therapists can sometimes inspire couples to reach for this lofty ideal by educating them to the awareness that self-transcendence, like true intimacy, is available only to those who are developmentally capable of setting ego aside to experience it. At the same time, it needs to be acknowledged that even the most mature among us cannot walk through life on the mountain tops without also wandering through the inevitable valleys of relationship pain and disappointment.

> The recognition that we are all fallible human beings means that we will err. To learn from our errors becomes a commitment to self-expansion and growth in deepening intimacy with another–a job of a lifetime. (Bernhard, 1996, p. 67)

Three truths beg to be stated: (1) No relationship will ever be perfect or perfectly intimate. (2) All relationships can become more intimate if the partners are willing to learn and grow. (3) If one partner is either unwilling or unable to grow, the other partner will need to decide to tolerate a life without intimacy, or to leave that relationship in search of a partner who is more mature. By daring to utilize theories and models that include moral and spiritual development as "lures to being" practitioners can become transformational influences for the couples and families with whom they work (Weinhold, 1989; Berenson, 1990; Weinhold & Hendricks, 1993; Kramer, 1995). However, self-transformation is a door that opens from the inside.

MENTORING THE NEXT GENERATION

It is important to consider the ways in which professional helpers can prepare the next generation to take its place in the world. Individuals can become more morally and spiritually mature only when they have access to the requisite knowledge, values and skills required. One way to facilitate that kind of awareness is for professional educators and therapists to learn and to teach more generous theories of human and family potential. When centered in a transpersonal context, relationships can be reframed as having a spiritual component (Hendrix, 1988). By learning how to identify joint goals that give both their lives more purpose and meaning, each member of the couple system can begin to heal the wounds of the past and move beyond egocentric life positions. Such growth in therapy is less likely when therapists fail to utilize transpersonal theories as catalysts for moral and spiritual development. Conversely, when a therapist models moral and spiritual values it brings a spiritual component into the therapeutic mix.

> If I believe that all life is connected in a kind of grand harmony, then I am going to look for ways that nudge the components of the human system, in my office on a given day, into the harmony that is inherently possible for us human inhabitants in the Great Web of Being. (Brothers, 1996, p. 5)

At its least effective moments, traditional therapy has too often opted to adjust a client or family system to the dominant culture's view of human potential, regardless of whether the culture's view was itself healthy or unhealthy, mature or immature. At its theoretical best, therapy should aim not simply to solve or ameliorate problems, but also to help clients transform old habits and ways of being to move beyond health and normality (Walsh & Shapiro, 1983) and toward the farther reaches of coupleship.

> Perhaps only a small percentage of couples will be able to live marriage as an alchemical relationship that helps them give birth to their finest qualities. Nonetheless, both history and evolution have shown many times that even a few pioneers can forge a new direction, which points the way for countless others. (Welwood, 1990, p. 199)

It has been posited that to facilitate optimum growth of individuals and systems, therapy needs to have a frame of reference that is bigger than its culture's (Tart, 1996). Transpersonal theories with their focus on moral and spiritual development can provide technologies for reaching the kind of developmental maturation required for healthy intimacy in relationships.

REFERENCES

Allport, G. (1959). Normative compatibility in the light of social science. In A. Maslow (Ed.), *New knowledge in human values.* New York: Harper & Row.

Basch, M. (1988). *Understanding psychotherapy: The science behind the art.* New York: Basic Books, Inc.

Bentz, V. (1989). *Becoming mature: Childhood ghosts and spirits in adult life.* New York: Aldine de Gruyter.

Berenson, D. (1990, Sept./Oct.). Spirituality and the limits of psychotherapy: Between I and thou. *Family Therapy Networker, 14*(5), 26-27.

Bernhard, Y. (1996). Virginia Satir's concepts of "styles of loving." In B.J. Brothers (Ed.), *Couples and the TAO of congruence.* New York: The Haworth Press, Inc.

Bettelheim, B. (1983). *Freud and man's soul.* New York: Alfred A. Knoff.

Bly, R. (1996). *The sibling society.* Reading, MA: Addison Wesley.

Bowen, M. (1976). Theory in the practice of psychotherapy. In P. Guerin (Ed.), *Family therapy: Theory and practice.* New York: Gardner Press, Inc.

Branden, N. (1982). Intensive workshop on self-esteem and romantic relationships. Beverly Hills, CA: Biocentric Institute.

Brothers, B.J. (Ed.) (1992). *Spirituality and couples: Heart and soul in the therapeutic process.* New York: The Haworth Press, Inc.

Bugental, E., & Bugental, J. (1984). Dispiritedness: A new perspective on a familiar state. *Journal of Humanistic Psychology, 24*(1), 49-27.

Chopra, D. (1997). *The path to love: Renewing the power of spirit in your life.* New York: Harmony Books.

Cowley, A. (1993). Transpersonal social work: A theory for the 1990s. *Social Work, 38*(5), 527-534.

Cowley, A., & Derezotes, D. (1994). Transpersonal psychology and social work education. *Journal of Social Work Education, 30*(1), 32-41.

Cowley, A. (1996). Transpersonal practice: A fourth force model. In F. Turner (Ed.) (4th Edition). *Social work treatment: Interlocking theoretical approaches.* New York: The Free Press, 663-698.

Cowley, A. (1999). Transpersonal theory and social work practice with couples and families. *Journal of Family Social Work, 3*(2), 5-22.

Erikson, W. (1950). *Childhood and society.* New York: W.W. Norton & Co., Inc.

Erikson, E., Erikson, J., & Kivnick, H. (1986). *Vital involvement in old age: The experience of old age in our time.* New York: W.W. Norton & Co., Inc.

Fromm, E. (1959). Values, psychology and human existence. In A. Maslow (Ed.), *New knowledge in human values.* New York: Harper & Row.

Gilligan, C. (1982). *In a different voice.* Cambridge, MA.: Harvard University Press.

Goldbart, S., & Wallen, D. (1994). *Mapping the terrain of the heart: The six capacities that guide the journey of love.* New York: Addison-Wesley.

Goldberg, C. (1980). *In defense of narcissism.* New York: Gardner Press.

Gould, R. (1978). *Transformations: Growth and change in adult life.* New York: Simon & Schuster, Inc.

Gurman, A. (1981). Integrative marital therapy: Toward the development of an interpersonal approach. In S. Budman (Ed.), *Forms of brief psychotherapy.* New York: Guilford.

Hendrix, H. (1988). *Getting the love you want: A guide for couples.* New York: Harper Perennial.

Heidegger, M. (1962). *Being and time.* New York: Harper & Row.

Horney, K. (1937). *The neurotic personality of our time.* New York: W.W. Norton.

Houston, J. (1982). *The possible human: A course in enhancing your physical, mental, and creative abilities.* Los Angeles: J.P. Tarcher.

Josselson, R. (1996). *The space between us: Exploring the dimensions of human relationships.* Thousand Oaks, CA: Sage.

Jourard, S. (1971). *The transparent self.* New York: Van Nostrand Reinhold.

Jung, C. (1933). *Modern man in search of a soul.* New York: Harcourt Brace.

Kegan, R. (1982). *The evolving self: Problem and process in human development.* Cambridge, MA: Harvard University Press.

Kernberg, O. (1980). *Internal world and external reality.* New York: Aronson.

Kohlberg, L. (1981). *The philosophy of moral development.* San Francisco: Harper & Row.

Korten, D. (1995/Summer). When corporations rule the world. *Noetic Sciences Review, 34,* 4-10.

Kramer, S. (1995). *Transforming the inner and outer family: Humanistic and spiritual approaches to mind-body-systems therapy.* New York: The Haworth Press, Inc.

Krueger, D. (1989). *Body self & psychological self: A developmental and clinical integration of disorders of the self.* New York: Brunner/Mazel.

Lasch, C. (1978). *The culture of narcissism: American life in an age of diminishing expectations.* New York: W.W. Norton.

Lifton, R. (1982). Beyond psychic numbing: A call to awareness. *American Journal of Orthopsychiatry, 52* (4), 619-629.

Maslow, A. (1959). *The farther reaches of human nature.* New York: Viking Compass Books.

Miller, M. (1995). *Intimate terrorism: The deterioration of erotic life.* New York: W.W. Norton.

Nichols, M. (1984). *Family therapy: Concepts and methods.* Boston: Allyn and Bacon.

Nichols, M. (1987). *The self in the system: Expanding the limits of family therapy.* New York: Brunner/Mazel.

Pine, F. (1985). *Developmental theory and clinical process.* New Haven: Yale University Press.

Rosen, H. (1988). The constructivist-developmental paradigm. In R. Dorfman (Ed.), *Paradigms of clinical social work.* New York: Brunner/Mazel, Inc., pp. 317-355.

Selman, R. (1971). Taking another's perspective: Role-taking development in early childhood. *Childhood Development, 42,* 1721-1734.

Sheehy, G. (1976). *Passages.* New York: E.P. Dutton & Co., Inc.

Simon, R. (1996/Sept./Oct.). Whatever happened to adulthood? *Networker, 78,* 54-62.

Steiner, C. (1981). *The other side of power: How to become powerful without being power-hungry.* New York: Grove Press, Inc.

Szent-Gyoergyi, A. (1974). Drive in living matter to perfect itself. *Synthesis, 1,* 14-26.

Tart, C. (1986). *Waking up: Overcoming the obstacles to human potential.* Boston: New Science Library/Shambhala.

Viorst, J. (1986). *Necessary losses: The loves, illusions, dependencies and impossible expectations that all of us have to give up in order to grow.* New York: Simon & Schuster.

Walsh, R., & Vaughn, F. (Eds.), (1980). *Beyond Ego: Transpersonal dimensions in psychology.* Los Angeles: J.P. Tarcher.

Walsh, R., & Shapiro, D. (Eds.), (1983). *Beyond health and normality: Explorations of exceptional psychological well-being.* New York: Van Nostrand Reinhold.

Wegscheider-Cruse, S. (1988). *Coupleship: How to build a relationship.* Deerfield Beach, FL: Health Communications, Inc.

Weinhold, B. (1989). Transpersonal theories in family treatment. In D. Fennel, & B. Weinhold (Eds.), *Counseling families.* Denver, CO: Love Publishing Co.

Weinhold, B., & Hendricks, G. (1993). *Counseling and psychotherapy: A transpersonal approach.* Denver, CO: Love Publishing Co.

Welwood, J. (1990). *Journey of the heart: Intimate relationship and the path of love.* New York: Harper Collins.

Wiches, F. (1966). *The inner world of childhood.* Englewood Cliffs, NJ: Prentice-Hall, Inc.

Wilber, K. (1986). The spectrum of development. In K. Wilber, J. Engler, & D. Brown (Eds.), *Transformations of consciousness.* Boston: New Science Library/ Shambhala.

Woolf, V. (1984). Good Life Seminar, by V. Vernon Woolf. Provo, Utah.

Reflections on Intimacy: A Path Toward Transformation of Self, Other and the Relationship

Liberty Kovacs

SUMMARY. Using the model of developmental stages of marriage as a framework, the author reflects on the unfolding of intimacy as the couple face the challenges that arise in the relationship. Each stage presents the couple with a particular theme, issue and conflict(s) that are not only rooted in the "unfinished business of the past" but are also connected to the transforming process of the evolving identities of self, other and the relationship. By confronting the changes and the tasks of each stage and integrating them with the growing identity, the couple attain deeper levels of closeness, constancy, mutuality and intimacy. *[Article copies available for a fee from The Haworth Document Delivery Service: 1-800-342-9678. E-mail address: <getinfo@haworthpressinc.com> Website: <http://www.HaworthPress.com>]*

Liberty Kovacs, PhD, has been a marital therapist for over 30 years and is in private practice in Sacramento, CA. She has taught at the University of California, San Francisco and Davis, and at California State University, Sacramento. She was a mental health consultant with the Community Mental Health Program in Sacramento County, and a clinician with the UCD Mental Health Service. She continues to teach workshops for couples based on her model of the six stages of marriage. This model was the subject of her Ph.D. dissertation from the California Graduate School of Family Psychology.

The author wishes to acknowledge and express her gratitude for the editorial assistance of Lynn Altizer, M.S., the computer expertise of Steven Courtney and Tim Taylor, and the support of Elisabeth Bower, M.S., and Rosalie Golub-Roth.

[Haworth co-indexing entry note]: "Reflections on Intimacy: A Path Toward Transformation of Self, Other and the Relationship." Kovacs, Liberty. Co-published simultaneously in *Journal of Couples Therapy* (The Haworth Press, Inc.) Vol. 9, No. 1/2, 2000, pp. 37-55; and: *Couples Connecting: Prerequisites of Intimacy* (ed: Barbara Jo Brothers) The Haworth Press, Inc., 2000, pp. 37-55. Single or multiple copies of this article are available for a fee from The Haworth Document Delivery Service [1-800-342-9678, 9:00 a.m. - 5:00 p.m. (EST). E-mail address: getinfo@haworthpressinc.com].

KEYWORDS. Couple dynamics and therapy, marital development, family psychology

Life has taught us that love does not consist in
gazing at each other but in looking outward
together in the same direction.

–Saint-Exupery, *Wind, Sand, Stars*

For marriage, which is always spoken of as a bond, becomes actually, in this stage, many bonds, many strands, of different texture and strength, making up a web that is taut and firm. The web is fashioned of love. Yes, many kinds of love: romantic love first, then, a slow-growing devotion and, playing through these, a constantly rippling companionship. It is made of many loyalties and interdependencies and shared experiences. It is woven of memories of meetings and conflicts; of triumphs and disappointments. It is a web of communication, a common language, and an acceptance of lack of language, too; a knowledge of likes and dislikes, of habits and reactions, both physical and mental. It is a web of instincts and intuitions, and known and unknown exchanges. The web of marriage is made of propinquity, in the day to day living side by side, looking outward in the same direction. It is woven in space and in time of the substance of life itself.

–Anne Morrow Lindberg, *Gift from the Sea*

In this paper, I shall be reflecting on what I have learned about intimacy in relationships as a practitioner in the field of marriage and family over the last thirty years. What follows in this paper is an integration of theories, concepts and research taken from five major disciplines–clinical psychology, psychiatry, family systems theories, family sociology and social psychology (Kovacs, 1982; 1983; 1988)–which I synthesized with my own clinical experience. The model of marriage (Kovacs, 1990; 1994; 1997; 1998) that I have used in my clinical work and in teaching couples in workshops was focused primarily on married couples. However, it has proven to be just as applicable with unmarried, cohabiting, remarried, gay and lesbian couples as well as business partners, co-worker, and friendship relationships.

This model, called an integrated developmental and family system model (Kovacs, 1988), views marriage as a separate phase of adult development that unfolds through stages over time with developmental tasks to be mastered at each stage. The cornerstone of human development is the separation-individuation process (Mahler, Pine and Bergman, 1975) which begins in infancy in relation to the mother-child (or significant surrogate). Development expands to include the father and other adults and children and continues in relation to peers, in adolescence. The psychic structures of the child's identity evolve out of this process. Later in adolescence and in adulthood this continuous differentiation process will be integrated with the past developmental accomplishments and consolidate the identity of the individual.

The differentiation process is one of the essential building blocks in the development of an enduring, reciprocal and intimate relationship (Edward, Ruskin and Turvini, 1981). This process establishes firm boundaries that will permit emotional intimacy, even merging, without fear of losing the self. Thus, the way the child experienced the separation-individuation process and the degree to which the child is able to develop a separate identity from that of the parents, sets the stage for future development and future relationships.

The tasks of each stage of development arise at certain periods of time (Kovacs, 1990; 1994; 1997). Successful achievement of the developmental tasks of each stage leads to a sense of accomplishment and esteem; failure in achieving such tasks delays the completion of subsequent tasks, resulting in the development of a variety of symptoms such as anxiety or depression. During transitions and stressful times, the uncompleted tasks (or "unfinished business") will arise again and signal that the tasks need to be completed. In clinical observations I have noted that transitions often revive or recapitulate past conflicts or problems and provide married couples with an opportunity to rework or complete the "unfinished business" of the past. When crises or transitions are reframed as "normal" occurrences in marriage, and described as an opportunity to change and grow, couples are motivated to work together in resolving differences. They can then proceed with the necessary work of their individual growth and development, and on redesigning the relationship to fit the growth needs of both partners and the relationship.

Theoretically, marital development would progress in an orderly, systematic and predictable manner over time. In reality, "getting stuck," i.e., falling into impasses and pitfalls–withdrawing or fleeing with increased tension, stress, and emotionality, is a common occurrence in the life of the marital pair.

The major thesis of the author's approach is that enduring, intimate relationships, such as marriage, become the context for adults to complete the "unfinished business" of the past and to achieve further differentiation and development as individuals and as a couple. By confronting the challenges of unresolved developmental and parental issues (sometimes, even, the unresolved issues in the parents' marriages) and unresolved family of origin issues that are evoked in the marital relationship, the couple discovers deepening levels of mutuality and intimacy.

EXPLORING INTIMACY

What is intimacy in relationships? When couples are asked what they want in their relationship, their responses are varied, yet, very similar: "I want more communication." "I want more closeness (or more time together)." "I want to share my feelings more," or "I want him to listen to me." There are the couples who want more (or less) sex, more time to have fun or more family time.

As I listen to their desires and dreams, I hear their yearnings for belonging, for the ability to express vulnerabilities and for "true love." Some partners can articulate a desire to be "truly myself" and to "know who I am." There are those who have achieved a level of independence in the relationship and state, "I want to be free," or "I want to have time alone," or "I want to be independent and still be accepted and welcomed back to the folds of the relationship." In these seemingly contradictory desires, couples are expressing the paradoxical aspects of love and intimacy in enduring relationships: closeness and time alone; the ability to share personal thoughts, feelings, and vulnerabilities while simultaneously desiring to be autonomous. What better definition of love is there than the spouse who says, "I want to love you as much as I love myself?" Here are the roots of intimacy: two unique individuals who want to commit their time and energy to the relationship in order to know, care about, and to share each other's lives.

We, human beings, need the trust and safety of a caring relationship and we need freedom of choice and decision-making as well as responsibility (as in, ability to respond) in order to grow a self–to become the person we were intended to be. All of these must happen for the relationship itself to continue evolving. Intimacy, then, is a complex, dynamic and progressive process which is necessary as a foundation of psychological growth and in transforming the evolving self, other, and the relationship.

Yet, relationships become battlegrounds of disappointment, disillusionment, and pain; relationships frequently are torn apart by the very same people who began with great love and hope when they fell in love. Rilke, a young German poet, told us nearly a hundred years ago:

> *. . . love is difficult. For one human being to love another: that is perhaps the most difficult of all our tasks, the ultimate, the last test and proof, the work for which all other work is but preparation.*[1]

In working with couples, I have found that by providing them with a map of the developmental stages of marriage (Marano, 1992), and by guiding them through their experiences in their relationship and in their families of origin, they can identify where they are "stuck" in their own development. Couples realize that the issues and conflicts with which they are struggling in their present relationship are similar to incidents and occurrences that happened in their parents' marriages. This is not to blame parents for their adult children's problems. Rather, I encourage the couple to identify the behavior patterns in their relationship that are represented by repetitive, intense emotions that are of long-standing duration. Such behavior signals that the source of their painful interactions are rooted in their past experiences.

Conflicts over money are very common. Jonathan and Sally had intense arguments over money. He saw her as careless or frivolous with money and unwilling to stay within the limits of their budget. Sally described his demands as unreasonable and "tight-fisted." She justified her spending by saying, "I'm using the money to buy necessities like groceries and clothes–clothes for children these days are not cheap; and I usually get only what they need."

My question at this point is: "How did you see your parents dealing with money?" Sometimes without hesitation, and sometimes at a slower pace, the couple will relate stories about their parents' interactions concerning the particular topic about which they have frequent arguments. In this instance, Jonathan revealed that his father did not manage money very well. His father had a tendency to buy "toys" when finances were tight and his mother was constantly juggling their funds to pay bills. Sally's parents had developed a more flexible approach to their budget which allowed her mother to buy "extras" occasionally.

This type of interplay between the present and past relationships is a large part of the therapeutic work that is done with couples until they can identify the patterns ("unfinished business from the past") and recognize that the repetitive nature of their interactions were learned in their families and brought into their relationship. Having mastered the ability to recognize these patterns, they are ready to shift their focus from blaming each other for their frustrations, to developing new ways of dealing with their particular problem or conflict. Only with this shift in perspective is the couple truly ready to "let go" of repetitive behavior patterns and to start working on redesigning and rebuilding their relationship together. The old patterns will emerge many times before the partners completely release old emotional reactions which are gradually replaced with more appropriate interactions.

COUPLE-THERAPIST COLLABORATING

The couple-therapist relationship is intended to be collaborative. From the first session, the spouses are encouraged to express their individual concerns and perceptions about their relationship and what each has done to solve the problem. In establishing a collaborative relationship, each person in the couple relationship will feel heard, understood, and accepted. I believe it is important from the very beginning to demonstrate acceptance of their differences and of their differentness. Emphasizing that each may have a different perspective of the way the relationship is functioning, as well as different ways of thinking, feeling and conducting their activities, removes the onus of having to be "right or wrong," or of blaming each other for their unhappiness in the relationship.

I explain to couples that they are "two different people who came from two different families and who learned two different ways of perceiving and behaving in the world." That each family is different is a theme that is reiterated throughout the therapy sessions. Each family has its own patterns of communication, way of showing affection, having fun, solving problems and resolving conflicts. Our task is to work together to redesign their relationship until it fits their needs and wants.

The theme of the differentness between the partners is reinforced by discussing their families of origin. Each partner is asked to create a family genogram, a diagram of their particular family. The diagramming of the families is done to demonstrate the idea that each partner came from a family with a different structure and process. The family genogram allows each spouse to understand the impact of their parent's marriage and family of origin.

Not only do I, the therapist, derive objective data from the use of the genogram, but the couple also becomes aware of multigenerational patterns. The family genogram is a valuable vehicle for disclosing triangular relationships, assumptions about roles (especially about marital roles), rules that were operating in each family regarding relationships, differing ways of expressing emotions, and in revealing wounds that were not healed in early efforts toward separation-individuation.

Concurrent with the creation of the family genogram, I also gather perceptual history data about the parents of each partner. Present day conflicts that arise in the therapy session can be traced back to the parents' marriages or the family structure. As time in therapy passes, each spouse and the therapist recognize the different ways that each family of origin functioned. When the family perceptual history and the family genogram are used in conjunction with the presenting problem(s), the couple dynamics are more readily identified by the therapist and the couple themselves. They now have a method for tracing multigenerational behavior patterns rather than blaming each other or their parents. Frequently, one or both spouses become so intrigued with family patterns that they explore family dynamics with other family members.

My working hypothesis is that the issue causing conflict between the pair, has its roots in the family of origin. My response to any intense emotional and repetitive pattern is to go back to the family genogram to identify the source: "How did you see your mothers and fathers (or other significant person) dealing with a similar issue?" In one instance, we discovered that a husband's withdrawal in a three-year marriage was based on his unresolved grief over the loss of his father and sister who were killed in an automobile accident when he was ten years old.

In another relationship in which one partner was having an affair, the other partner remembered that at the age of six he discovered his mother with her lover. In the couple therapy, he was able to confront his acknowledged feelings from childhood, as well as his wife's affair. As noted above, unresolved parental issues, such as secret affairs, are carried into, and reenacted in the marriages of adult children.

Thus, very early in the therapy sessions, each spouse becomes aware of his or her family structure, process and dynamics, and of their parents' models of marriage. It becomes obvious to the couple and to the therapist how the family of origin and the parents' models of marriage have influenced their own interactions in their marriage. We also review how each progressed through his/her individual stages of development as infants, children and adolescents. Through this process of sharing their issues and conflicts with each other, couples not only see and reexperience their individual childhood patterns that are being reenacted in the marriage, they also plant the seeds of empathy and compassion toward each other that continue to grow as they learn to share their lives with each other.

In addition to examining family dynamics and childhood pattern, the therapist teaches and demonstrates the tools the couple practices with each other outside the therapy sessions. These tools are: communication, problem-solving, conflict resolution, negotiation, and empathy-building skills. The therapy session becomes a laboratory to practice the missing skills. For example, couples who blame each other for problems will frequently make "you" statements in the session. I interrupt such statements and recommend that they substitute "I" statements in expressing their thoughts or feelings. With practice in the therapy sessions and at home, couples change the way they are communicating. I use a similar approach for problem-solving or conflict-resolution skills: I focus on a problem the couple is having (or a conflict) and take them through the problem-solving and conflict resolution steps until they are familiar enough with the process that they begin to use it at home.

In the following sections, I will map out the development of the marriage and how it unfolds through the stages with the tasks to be mastered at each stage, and how intimacy is manifested at each stage.

STAGE I–HONEYMOON

The first stage has been called the honeymoon stage, romance and fantasy time. The Greeks called this time of being in love (or Eros) "a divine state of madness." It is characterized by a highly romanticized, idealized and exclusive relationship. This is a highly sexualized state that brings two people to the height of emotional intensity and infatuation where they want nothing more than to be with each other forever. They feel that all their needs are being fulfilled and both are giving and receiving effortlessly. All they want is to be in each other's presence. The myth is that this love will last forever.

However, the reality is that this is an unconscious choice and a temporary experience. Generally, falling in love is considered a genetically determined and an instinctual aspect of mating behavior and suited for the perpetuation of the species. Yet, in our society, falling in love is considered the first step toward developing an enduring, committed relationship. The ability to merge–to become "one" and connect deeply–is necessary for establishing a boundary around each other. The relationship is also necessary to initiate the psychological work of expanding each one's identity through the awakening of a dormant part of the personality–the part that needs love and affection. From my perspective, in the act of falling in love, the couple is building a reservoir, metaphorically, in which to store their powerful emotions and passions; thereafter, this reservoir becomes a source of love and affection when the relationship runs dry or becomes distant and disengaged.

The major tasks of the honeymoon stage involves: (1) building a foundation for a mutually gratifying, caring and supportive relationship, separate from the family of origin. The exclusivity of this stage is important for achieving a sense of belonging and for developing trust in each other's commitment to an evolving relationship; (2) establishing the beginnings of the relationship boundary that are clear enough to permit the growth of an intimate relationship separate from the family of origin, as well as permit the growth of the two individuals who make up the relationship; (3) providing for the optimal level of nurturance that each person needs. This is achieved through the emotional intensity of this stage. When that level of nurturance has been achieved, the couple is ready to move on to the next stage.

The intimacy at this level is experienced in the passion, sensuality and sexuality of two who are one–who seem to think, feel and act as one. They give and receive without effort. There is a magical and mythical air about them; they are in a world of their own. "I've never felt like this before." "I feel complete." "I'm happier than I've ever been." Falling in love takes the two to the heights of feeling and imagination. Time stands still. They experience great surges of energy and excitement and all they want is to be together. When they are apart, all they can think about is the beloved.

Yet, time and life do not stand still. In reality this cocoon-like existence–this exquisite state of nurturance–will reach satiation, and one or both will begin to move toward differentiation and the next stage of marriage. The transition toward the next stage is characterized by disappointment and disillusionment by one partner when the other wants to do something different or separate from his/her partner. This first step toward growth is painful and is frequently met with resistance and conflict.

STAGE II–EXPECTATIONS

The intense closeness and symbiosis gradually give way to reality which cannot be denied forever. The complex issues of living together, increasing responsibilities and problems begin to intrude. The couple will struggle to accommodate, to compromise and to use whatever strategies are necessary to maintain harmony and eliminate disagreements. However, the more the conflicts are avoided–are not dealt with constructively so both people may learn with each other–the more stagnant and static the relationship becomes.

The tasks of the second stage are complex and difficult: (1) the couple will continue relinquishing the fantasies of an all-encompassing lover who will fulfill all their needs, and start accepting the idea that each will provide for his/her own needs in life; (2) new patterns of relating to each other will be worked out. Each partner can allow self/partner time to be alone, apart from each other. They begin re-establishing contacts with friends, family and co-workers, as well as enjoying activities together; (3) the couple will begin reconciling their different styles and their expectations of each other as husband and wife, and begin seeing each other as adults–not parent/child. This requires being able to say what each wants or needs; (4) they will learn to compromise, in order to meet adult goals, responsibilities; (5) they will learn to balance multiple roles as husband/wife, mother/father, son/daughter, worker/friend; (6) the rules of the relationship will be worked out and they will learn to deal with tensions and conflicts that develop while still maintaining closeness and connnectedness.

Issues of differentiation take time to negotiate and require a review of each family of origin and exploration of how each family handled differentness, differences and rules about disagreements. The expectations of husband and wife roles were derived from their parents' models of marriage. These expectations must be modified or changed to fit the reality of who they are as a couple in the present. The roles their parents created for themselves may not be appropriate for their adult children. The couple has to work out their own way of fulfilling their mutual goals and responsibilities in the relationship.

The quality of intimacy–the emotional intensity, exclusivity and merging–begins to change in the second stage. The couples will struggle to hold on to the intimacy they have known, but intimacy changes as they realize that they are not exactly alike–that they do have different interests and different ways of thinking, feeling and conducting activities. Simultaneously, the couple is also realizing the extent of their needs for other relationships with family, friends, and co-workers.

Instead of grasping for the intimacy they have known in the previous stage, couples let go of their fantasies about each other and confront the reality of their disappointment and disillusionment. This is a time of sharing their vulnerabilities and working together in learning how they are different and who they are as individuals with their own strengths and limitations and their differing needs and wants. This is a time for sharing their pain, comforting each other and being open to another level of intimacy that is growing.

I have observed couples in therapy who have been married from one to over thirty years who have not confronted their disappointment because of fearing to hurt each other. When couples cannot share their hurt and disappointment with each other, the damage done to the intimacy in the relationship is observable and palpable as evidenced in their distant and angry interactions. With gentle encouragement to express the feelings that they had never dared to tell each other, the response is one of immediate relief, as if a terrible burden were lifted. With the barrier removed, the couple experiences more openness and a more freely given affection.

The couple learns in this stage that intimacy means more than romance and sexuality. Their perception of intimacy expands to include sharing their disappointments, pain and vulnerabilities. By acknowledging and affirming each other's individuality and differentness, they are moving toward the third stage of marital development and another challenge to their growing intimacy.

STAGE III–POWER STRUGGLE

At this time, the relationship is characterized by a growing divergence of interests and movement toward more assertive, autonomous behavior, usually on the part of one spouse more than the other. The accommodation of the earlier years has all but disappeared. The assertive one will appear to be testing, experimenting with trials of new behaviors: "I want to do this a different way and see what happens." "Will I be accepted?" The focus is on finding one's strengths, abilities, capacities (power base) in relation to one's partner without resulting in one dominating and the other submitting. One will tug in one direction and find the other pulling in a different direction. Arguments break out over "silly," inconsequential matters, at first, then, more serious issues: sex, money, disciplining the children, or the in-laws.

The important power struggle tasks to be achieved at this stage in the relationship include: (1) developing the structures in the relationship that will allow for shared responsibilities, decision-making together and separately, and managing household tasks, finances, and child-rearing practices; (2) expanding the boundaries of the relationship so each partner will bring forth the hidden aspects of self into full view, and provide each room for testing or experimenting with new roles or positions that each may take in relation to the other; (3) reinforcing the foundation of support, empathy and connectedness by sharing the wounded aspects of their lives with each other, and accepting the positive and negative traits of the partner and self; (4) attaining a balance of power in an atmosphere of trust in which each may express his/her own abilities and each is acknowledged and appreciated for the contributions made in working together.

Intimacy seems to be a contradiction at this stage of marital development. The relationship is becoming a testing ground for each spouse to assert him/herself in making decisions, in determining how the relationship will be structured and how tasks will be shared and completed. The struggles to resolve these issues are manifested in a range of interactions: from silence and withdrawal to tugs-of-war to polarization and all-out battles (in some relationships deteriorating to verbal and physical abuse). The marriage at this point appears to be heading for chaos and self-destruction.

During this critical time, the couple is testing the trust, love, and acceptance that they have for each other and the relationship. They shed their facades and armor and allow more of the true self to show itself. Yet, for two people who love and respect each other and who want to be together in a sharing and freely giving and receiving environment, the choice is paradoxical: In order to feel accepted, one must allow him/herself to become more vulnerable to the other–to show a softer, or alternately, a more independent side, of one's self.

Yes, this is the risk: to reveal unexposed aspects of one's true self, with no attempt to control or overpower the other to get one's own way. For intimacy to grow each must find the capacity to respond to the other's pain with understanding and empathy. To achieve this more intimate relationship with each other, the couple must risk more open communication with each other, more willingness to negotiate their differences and to work cooperatively. They must also learn that conflict is not to be feared, and to see it as an opportunity to learn more about self and other; and that differences or differentness can be viewed as enhancing the relationship rather than being a threat or a rejection. The transition toward the next stage occurs when the partners relinquish the power struggles and move towards cooperation and intimacy.

STAGE IV–THE SEVEN-YEAR-ITCH

The more the self is manifested, the more conflict and turmoil the couple experiences. By this stage in the relationship, the couple realizes that conflict is a signal that a change is about to happen, and both are open to learning from the experience. This fourth stage tests the limits of their capacity to love and accept each other; in this stage the unfinished issues around dependence/independence emerge. It is, therefore, one of the most stressful times for couples, particularly, when adolescent children are in the family. One or both parents are re-living adolescent struggles, and often midlife crises as well, at a time when their own children are in the throes of their own struggles.

At a time when couples need each other for stability, one or both are deeply involved in completing the tasks of individuation and midlife: (1) achieving separateness/independence *and* the ability to reconnect without losing one's identity; (2) achieving improved negotiation skills and improving skills of conflict resolution by learning from the push-pull of the relationship; (3) consciously choosing the relationship as a way of life.

Intimacy seems practically non-existent at this point in the relationship. The cries for more freedom, more independence and more separateness are loud and clear. In fact, the discussions of separation and divorce are increasing. The chasm between the pair seems impassable. The focus on the individual needs of each member–to "finding my self"–this may mean finding fulfillment outside the relationship in new jobs, promotions, and travel. There may even be affairs which are distractions from the work of individuation that is necessary at this time. Still there are yearnings to get together sexually or socially.

Paradoxically, the best treatment for assisting couples who want to save their marriage is the structured trial separation (Kovacs, 1994; 1998). The separation is intended as a prevention of further erosion of the relationship and to provide the couple with a "breathing space." The mention of a separation is so anxiety-provoking for couples in earlier stages of marriage that they flee into their dysfunctional patterns of behavior at the mention of a separation. Their reactions to the suggestion of a separation is indicative of couples in earlier stages of marriage who have not achieved the level of individuation for more separateness. Even in the fourth stage, the therapist will explore with each spouse how they handled their independence issues with their parents during adolescence. Those who used flee tactics (i.e., they left home early "to get away from home" by getting married after graduation from high school, or went to work), may be repeating an old pattern of unresolved issues with parents. These issues will need to be explored thoroughly before a trial separation takes place.

Kirschner and Kirschner (1986, p. 167) stated that "fear-of-loss tactics have been used by spouses to discipline each other in normal family life" when they are struggling with separation. These authors have described several levels of maneuvers that couples use along a continuum of potency: from the least potent where couples refuse to speak to each other to the next level when the husband or wife may sleep in separate bedrooms and refuse to have sex to the next level when one partner is threatening to have an affair or to separate. The most potent maneuvers are actual separation, initiating divorce proceedings and, finally, divorce.

In my practice I have seen many couples who have used most, and sometimes all of the above tactics, in attempts to bring the independent partner back into the former positions in the relationship. Paradoxically, I have found that a structured trial separation (Granvold, 1983; Kovacs, 1994; 1998) is very effective in assisting couples who want to save their marriage at this stage and to prevent further deterioration of the marriage. During the separation each partner gains a more realistic perspective of the marriage and they realize that they want to stay in the relationship. The risk of divorce is there too, and the couple is encouraged to express their fears and concerns. An essential element is continued therapy in which the therapist guides and facilitates the process with the individuals and the relationship. More often than not, the trial separation provides an opportunity to examine their needs and wants and to consider the changes that each is willing to ask for and to make.

The most significant learning experience at this time comes from focusing on the unexpressed needs or wants of the partners; as one client told me, "I didn't realize I had a need to be alone until we separated. Now, I know how to ask for what I want." This comment is reminiscent of Rilke's recommendation for a loving relationship "*in which one appoints the other guardian of his solitude and show him this confidence, the greatest in his power to bestow. . . . Once the realization is accepted that even between the closest human beings infinite distances can exist, a wonderful living side by side can grow up, if they succeed in loving the distance between them which makes it possible to see each other whole and against a wide sky!*"[2]

Poets and artists have been telling us for many generations that love and intimacy grow when each person has attained a constancy of self–when each can contain one's own identity and be responsible for one's own life. Only then can one individual consciously choose to share his life with another.

STAGE V–RECONCILIATION

When each member of the couple relationship has achieved a sense of constancy–"I am I and you are you"–the fifth stage begins. Stage five is characterized by active efforts toward understanding and accepting that the strivings for independence are "normal" growth efforts rather than rejection. The self and other are viewed more realistically. They are more accepting of each other's and their own, limitations and they express more appreciation of each other's strengths and those of the relationship.

There is a greater willingness to take responsibility for one's own needs, wants, thoughts, and feelings and to accept the fact that each is unique and different. Perceived differences are now viewed as an enhancement of the marital relationship rather than a threat. The couple accepts dependent and independent needs and there is more sharing of responsibilities, tasks, decision-making, and planning for the future.

The tasks for this stage are reinforcing and strengthening of earlier ones. These are: (1) achieving a clear sense of self and other; (2) choosing the relationship as a way of life; (3) taking responsibility for one's self and freely sharing one's self with the other; (4) sharing responsibilities of daily living, and supporting each other's strengths and successes; and (5) recognizing and accepting each other's interdependence.

Intimacy at this stage is expressed in celebrations with friends and family. Vows are renewed, honeymoon sites are revisited or they take the honeymoon they never had. Second honeymoons are consciously planned and enjoyed. Renewal is the theme at this stage. The couple is happy with each other, more openly affectionate and caring about each other. There is more autonomy in the relationship. Communication is more improved and direct. Collaboration increases. Problems, conflicts, and difficulties are confronted earlier and handled through negotiation. The couple is more reality-oriented and experiences a high level of warmth, love, and intimacy with consideration given to the other's needs and wants as well as one's own. This stage is described as commitment, freedom and together again. This is "one of the best times of life," for they are together as a couple and they have a strong sense of their individual identities as well.

STAGE VI–ACCEPTANCE

Now the relationship flows quite naturally. Stage six is a period of resolution and integration. It is ushered in by mutual acceptance; the couple has stopped wondering what the other is thinking or feeling and stopped trying so hard to please, because they feel fully accepted and fully accepting. This is a time of surging personal growth. Both partners are free to explore new ways of fulfilling themselves as individuals and as a couple. They can focus more time and energy on giving to others, to social and political causes or to pursuing artistic and spiritual interests.

The tasks of this stage are more reality-based depending on the age of the couple: (1) accepting graciously the passing of time and the aging process as well as preparing for middle-age/elderhood changes which include planning for job changes, retirement, travelling and maintaining health needs; (2) facing the losses inherent in the aging process: parents, friends, spouse and finding satisfactory sources of affection, closeness, and belonging; (3) simplifying one's life and developing or maintaining a spiritual base for one's continued growth and development; (4) preparing for eventual and inevitable cessation of life.

CONCLUSION

The developmental view of marriage is not a static arrangement between two unchanging people. The psychological tasks of the marital couple are more dynamic and complex than is generally recognized by the ecstatic couple who enters this relationship believing that "love conquers all" and will result in "living happily ever after."

In an enduring, intimate relationship, the pair will realize that it takes time and work to learn to love the person with whom one falls in love–to love the real person, not the romantic fantasy. One task of marriage at every stage is raising one's consciousness of what it means to be a couple–to become an intimate couple each must first become an integrated and whole individual.

Each must also become increasingly aware of what he/she contributes to the tensions, stress, and conflicts in the relationship and to take ownership of such contributions; otherwise, the relationship becomes mired in repression, projection, and stagnation. The family of origin of each partner has significant influence in their marriage through the basic parent-child relationship, the parent's model of marriage, and through the family dynamics. This model of marital development does not place blame on the parents or the family, but rather it takes into account their influence in the relationship. This understanding is important in making the necessary changes and in redesigning the marriage to fit the couple not the family of origin.

In our society of mass media fantasizing, couples who want an intimate, enduring relationship will soon realize that in addition to the basic tools of marriage mentioned above, they will need additional tools. These tools–discipline, commitment, and conscious love–permit the couple to grow beyond uncontrolled emotions and becomes a love that cherishes, cares for and about the other, and the self. This love strengthens both partners in containing and facing their vulnerabilities and in sharing their disappointments, hurts, and pain with each other.

This model of marriage views enduring relationships as the context for the continued psychological and spiritual transformation of the selfhood of two individuals who will plan, design, and maintain a couple relationship. This relationship must be flexible and expansive enough to contain the paradoxical yearnings of both people–togetherness/separateness; autonomy/belongingness; dependence/independence. Ultimately, the couple will achieve interdependence, mutuality, and intimacy. The challenge of the marital process is to balance the strivings for individuality and togetherness simultaneously while living in an enduring, intimate relationship.

NOTES

1. Rilke, R. M. (1993) *Rilke on Love and Other Difficulties* (Translations and Considerations by John J. L. Mood). New York: W. W. Norton & Company, p. 31.
2. Ibid., p. 28

REFERENCES

Edward, J., Ruskin, W., & Turvini, P. (1981). *Separation-individuation: Theory and application* (p. 107). New York: Gardner Press.

Granvold, D. (1983). Structured Separation for marital treatment and decision-making. *Journal of Marital and Family Therapy,* 9(4), 403-412.

Kirschner, D. A., and Kirschner, S. (1986). *Comprehensive family therapy an integration of systemic and psychodynamic treatment models.* New York: Brunner/Mazel, Publishers.

Kovacs, L. (1982). Development of the Marital Relationship (dissertation). Ann Arbor, MI: University Microfilms International.

Kovacs, L. (1983). A conceptualization of marital development. *Family Therapy,* 10, (3), 183-210.

Kovacs, L. (1988). Couple therapy: An integrated developmental and family system model. *Family Therapy,* 15 (2), 133-155.
Kovacs, L. (1990). Today's marriage: The six stages. A videotape produced by author.
Kovacs, L. (1994). Separateness/Togetherness: A paradox in relationships. *Journal of Couple Therapy,* 4, 3/4, 88-94; and: *Surpassing threats and rewards* (ed: Barbara Jo Brothers) The Haworth Press, Inc., 1994, pp. 83-94.
Kovacs, L. (1997). The power struggle stage: From polarization to empathy. *Journal of Couple Therapy,* 7, 1, 27-37; and: *When one partner is willing and the other is not* (ed. Barbara Jo Brothers) The Haworth Press, Inc., 1997, pp. 27-37.
Kovacs, L. (1998). Structured trial separation. In L. L. Hecker, S. A. Deacon, and Associates (Eds.), *The therapist's handbook homework, handouts and activities for use in psychotherapy.* New York: The Haworth Press, Inc., pp. 177-184.
Mahler, M., Pine, F., & Bergman, A. (1975). *The psychological birth of the human infant symbiosis and individuation.* New York: Basic Books.
Marano, H. E. (Jan./Feb.,1992). The reinvention of marriage. *Psychology Today.*

From Projective Identification to Empathic Connection: The Transformation of a Marriage from the Inside Out

Arthur G. Mones
Frank Patalano

SUMMARY. This article examines the challenging journey of successful coupling by understanding the marital relationship within a developmental framework. The process of Projective Identification is viewed as a useful concept found at the confluence of family systems and psychodynamic streams of thought, bridging the interpersonal and intrapsychic experience of couples whose individuative strivings are stalled. A map is offered for the transformation of a marriage from the stages of Idealization and Disillusionment toward the stage of Acceptance and empathic connection. *[Article copies available for a fee from The Haworth Document Delivery Service: 1-800-342-9678. E-mail address: <getinfo@haworthpressinc.com> Website: <http://www.HaworthPress.com>]*

KEYWORDS. Projective identification, stages of marriage, couples therapy

---

Arthur G. Mones, PhD, is Coordinator, Specialization in Family and Marital Therapy, Center for Psychological Services and Clinical Studies, St. John's University.

Frank Patalano, PhD, is Associate Professor of Clinical Psychology, Department of Psychology, St. John's University.

Address correspondence to: Dr. Arthur G. Mones, Center for Psychological Services and Clinical Studies, St. John's University, 8000 Utopia Parkway, Jamaica, NY 11439.

[Haworth co-indexing entry note]: "From Projective Identification to Empathic Connection: The Transformation of a Marriage from the Inside Out." Mones, Arthur G., and Frank Patalano. Co-published simultaneously in *Journal of Couples Therapy* (The Haworth Press, Inc.) Vol. 9, No. 1/2, 2000, pp. 57-66; and: *Couples Connecting: Prerequisites of Intimacy* (ed: Barbara Jo Brothers) The Haworth Press, Inc., 2000, pp. 57-66. Single or multiple copies of this article are available for a fee from The Haworth Document Delivery Service [1-800-342-9678, 9:00 a.m. - 5:00 p.m. (EST). E-mail address: getinfo@haworthpressinc.com].

INTRODUCTION

Approximately one-half of marriages in the United States end in divorce. Moreover, most studies report that almost sixty percent of second marriages fail (Carter & McGoldrick, 1989; Gottman, 1994; Hetherington, Law, & O'Connor, 1993; Peck & Manocherian, 1989). Inasmuch as marriage is the centerpiece of family life and families make up the fabric of our society, it is important to study the intrapsychic, interpersonal and intergenerational aspects of what goes wrong in these partnerships and, more importantly, what can work successfully in a marriage. (Note: the term "marriage" in this paper is applicable to same sex partnerships and committed couples in cohabitation.) This paper will attempt to present a map for charting the course of marriage and a formula for navigating the challenging journey of successful coupling. The theoretical base for this model will be broad and integrative in nature, borrowing from psychoanalytic, family systems and behavioral conceptualizations. The authors believe strongly in melding concepts from these models so that therapeutic work can become enhanced for the front-line clinician. We hope to place the useful concept of projective identification within a family systems context in a way that will result in a strengthening of the efficacy of psychodynamic and family systems approaches to work with couples. We view this term as located at the confluence of these theoretical streams of thought, and, as such, is a useful process for enhancing the challenging work of marital therapy.

DEVELOPMENTAL STAGES OF MARRIAGE AND ROLE OF PROJECTIVE IDENTIFICATION

Marriages progress through identifiable developmental stages (Nadelson, Polonsky & Mathews, 1984; Jacobson & Christensen, 1996; Scarf, 1987). Typically, in being launched into the responsibilities of young adulthood, two people are full of aspiration and hope. This hopefulness, however, is accompanied by being emotionally incomplete. This incompleteness is fraught with anxiety at times so great that the launching stage can be rendered quite stressful or even aborted. This can be seen in adolescents or young adults who turn to drugs, promiscuity, criminality or even experience a psychotic process such that they are unable to successfully leave home and successfully navigate the developmental course of their lives (Haley, 1980). Those individuals who are able to progress into psychological adulthood move forward and attempt to complete their education and begin their careers still containing a great deal of anxiety regarding their lack of emotional completeness. As Erikson (1950, 1979) indicates, young adults at this stage of their development are actively seeking out a partner who will provide a sense of intimacy and psychological completeness. The selection of the partner is a complex, multi-determined process. To a great extent, this choice is an unconscious one, influenced by the individual's prior significant relationships and internalized working models. Most often, we find a partner who allows us to feel wonderful, whole and in love with life. We experience this coupling as immeasurably exciting and, at the same time, significantly anxiety-reducing. The relationship enables us to feel safe and secure. This is called the stage of Idealization (Nadelson, Polonsky & Mathews, 1984). In this stage similarities are emphasized and differences are minimized or denied altogether. This "honeymoon period" is quite romantic as is expressed in popular music of all eras with themes such as, "Now that I've found you my life is wonderful" or the sadder (blues) version, "Without you I am a lost person," etc.

While the process of Projective Identification is typically described as an externalization of unwanted or uncomfortable aspects of the person (Klein, 1946; Scharff & Scharff, 1991, 1992), we hold that projections of hope, healing, and completeness can likewise occur within intimate relationships. In a sense, both ends of the emotional spectrum can be projected onto the partner in the service of seeking feelings of psychological completeness and emotional invulnerability, driven by the frightening existential awareness of our finite nature (Becker, 1973).

Sooner or later, there is a realization, albeit largely unconscious, that the sense of incompleteness, sadness and pain cannot be erased or soothed fully via the relationship with the other person. This dynamic becomes played out by each partner feeling increasingly disappointed in regard to the experienced imperfections and flaws of the other. This felt sense of internal agitation and frustration is externalized and projected onto the partner who is now blamed for being the source of misery and dissatisfaction. This is the Disillusionment Stage (Nadelson, Polonsky, & Mathews, 1984) wherein differences are magnified and similarities minimized. Partners increasingly doubt the sagacity of their union. Is this what marriage was supposed to be? Did I make a wrong choice? Just as the partner was credited with the glowing feelings during Idealization, now the mate may be actively blamed for creating a marital climate of deeply felt unhappiness. On different levels of consciousness, there is an awareness that, indeed, one's sense of psychological incompleteness still exists. There is a great deal of anxiety experienced at the awesome responsibility of individuation (or differentiation) of Self (Bowen, 1978; Schnarch, 1991). The management of this very difficult internal state of incompleteness and anxiety takes the form of blame of the other. Each partner casts blame upon the other and makes attempts to pressure and force the mate to change. These attempts at forcing change only engender a greater degree of conflict and anger. Anger begets anger, and, under coercion, human beings dig their heels in further, resisting change and further accuse the other person of inadequacies (Mones & Panitz, 1994). As these accusatory interactions escalate, they result in greater and greater polarization between the couple (Jacobson & Christensen, 1996). Arguments ensue, making it increasingly difficult for partners to communicate on a reciprocally mature and humane level. As articulated by Gordon (1990), each spouse will feel that, "If we disagree, one of us must be wrong. I cannot tolerate the experience of myself being in the wrong (vulnerable), so it must be my partner who has a mistaken view, behavior, etc. I must prove this to be the case (in order to protect myself from feelings of inadequacy)."

Such is the drama of the Disillusionment Phase. What is described above is an integrative view of Projective Identification, taken from systems and psychodynamic conceptualizations. It is a process in which unwanted and intolerable feelings about Self are externalized onto another human being specifically, in this case, the person who was previously experienced as making his/her mate so complete and happy. Unlike an accurate empathic identification with the other, the projective identification usually significantly distorts the behavior, attitudes, feelings, and intentions of the partner (Grotstein, 1981). This distortion is fueled by a protection of intolerable feelings of sadness, hurt and fear within each of the partners. From a realistic point of view, as one or both spouses begin to think that the marriage has been a mistake, the desire for the fruits of the stage of Idealization returns. This may lead many to consider the possibility of choosing a new partner, one who will restore that wonderful feeling. For many, this "emotional logic" leads to divorce. Unfortunately, this decision often leads to a repeat performance, i.e., a second marriage or relationship that, once again, travels from Idealization to Disillusionment and ends in failure. This may explain the current seemingly high statistic of second marriages ending in divorce sixty percent of the time (Carter & McGoldrick, 1988; Hetherington, Law, & O'Connor, 1993; Gottman, 1994; Peck & Manocherian, 1989). Often, love is not so wonderful the second time around.

Many couples who decide to maintain their marriage tend to live out a lifetime of oscillation between Idealization and Disillusionment. Such a couple will continually enter a phase of intense mutual blame and discontent, followed by a period of "making up" and romanticism in a recursive cycle. Such relationships can be likened to a gambler's fallacy, that is, "I will learn to tolerate the losses and bad times because I know that, periodically, there are bound to be good times and positive payoffs down the road." Students of learning psychology know that intermittent reinforcement is the most powerful strategy for maintaining behavior. Individuals with severe trauma in their family of origin history tend to idealize to a greater degree in an often desperate attempt to feel repaired and to avoid intense internal emotional pain. This process may help to explain why 55% of battered women stay with their abusing spouses (Walker, 1991).

What then is the healthier alternative? Is it possible for the individuals in a relationship to become liberated from the vicious cycle of unproductive choices as outlined above? There is, for some couples, the ability to progress to another phase, one that is inherently healthy and fulfilling for the individuals and for the relationship (McAdams, 1989). Some couples are able to attain this higher stage of marital development via a continuing process of emotional growth and maturation. Others can be guided to this stage with the help of marital therapy.

The stage of more mature, healthier marital relating is called Acceptance (Jacobson & Christensen, 1996). It evolves when the members of a relationship come to the realization that the partner is not solely responsible for producing one's state of unhappiness, and, for that matter, not solely responsible for producing happiness. That is to say that, essentially, each partner owns the responsibility for his/her process of individuation, development, and actualization (Bowen, 1978;

Schnarch, 1991). This realization requires the genuine acknowledgment and admission by each partner that he/she is an imperfect, fallible human being, burdened by insecurity and anxiety regarding their psychological functioning, safety, and well-being. As the partners are able to own this painful reality and, in turn, to courageously share this awareness openly, a new, deeper, and more meaningful relationship emerges. In this more mature coupling, there is an understanding of each other and a growing attunement and sensitivity to each other's limitations and strivings. In essence, there is an empathic connection. Within this new stage of Acceptance, there is no longer the need to paper over differences (as in Idealization) or to distort and vilify the other for being deficient (as in Disillusionment). Projective Identification in the service of protecting against the experience of emotional incompleteness recedes as understanding and empathy play a more dominant role. Now differences can more and more be appreciated as aspects of the partner's unique psychological individuation and sense of self. These differences do not have to lead to emotional distance and polarization, as they did in the past. Moreover, because of the more accurate empathic connections that are developing, the partners can more realistically step into each other's shoes to understand the needs, expectations, intentions, and behaviors of each other. Some couples can actually become closer in the process of safely dealing with differences and validating each other's right to their feelings. This is the enormous power of intimacy.

TREATMENT CONSIDERATIONS

In regard to marital therapy, how does the therapist work with a couple in helping them move toward the stage of Acceptance? Firstly, the therapist will help the couple become aware of and "appreciate" frustration, anxiety and anger as signals that something is wrong. The therapist directs the partners to become increasingly aware of the sources of these irritations, helping them to gradually work through and let go of angry recriminations and externalizations of blame. Each partner, will, over time, be helped to take responsibility for his/her own vulnerability and the embedded fear, sadness and hurt carried from family-of-origin experience, along with other life disappointments, past and present. Each will be encouraged and prodded to put his/her Self in an individuating, leadership position, both intrapsychically and interpersonally (Schwartz, 1995). Skills of listening, talking, and communication will be taught and monitored (Markman, Stanley, & Blumberg, 1994). An important agent for change is the partners' growing sense of identification with and emulation of the way in which the therapist empathically listens, talks, and communicates. The partners are able to internalize some of the more adaptive, reality-based, emotionally mature attributes of a new working model, the therapist (Kissen, 1996; Patalano, 1997; Siegel, 1991). If the therapist's interventions are presented within the context of the empathic connection, these skills are more likely to be effectively learned, valued and operationalized by the couple. These skills, in turn, reinforce, strengthen, and consolidate the field of empathy and lead to true teamwork for the couple. The process of intimately relating becomes the dominant operative mode rather than the win-lose mentality of earlier times. In other words, the means become as important as the ends in dealing with inevitable disagreement and conflict. The emotional climate can now take on a real quality of mutual empathic attunement that is quite different from the extreme emotional positions associated with the stages of Idealization and Disillusionment. Problems in living become just that, challenges and issues to be discussed, negotiated, understood, and worked through rather than triggers for intrapsychic pain, interpersonal struggle, and marital discontent.

CASE EXAMPLE

Gene (38), married Bea (45), following the breakup of Bea's first marriage. Gene worked as a state employee while Bea was employed as a medical secretary. There were two children from Bea's previous marriage. As both of Gene's parents were alcoholic and depressed, he and his older two siblings were exposed to episodic explosiveness, criticism, and verbal abuse punctuated by periods of seeming calm and "normality." Significant to Bea's history was her placement in foster care from birth to five years of age at which time she and a younger sister were adopted into the same family. Gene was in recovery from alcohol abuse and was an active participant in Alcoholics Anonymous. Bea was a committed member of Alanon.

The beginning phase of this relationship found both partners powerfully in love. Bea was very attracted to Gene's ability to be quite nurturing to her children. Gene felt the security of Bea's level of high functioning and take charge manner. There was, in fact, an intensely felt period of Idealization. However, as several years elapsed, Bea's super-responsible, overfunctioning style of behavior that developed during her formative years as an adaptation to a fundamental emotional insecurity, began to trigger a depression and withdrawal in Gene. This stirred up a sense of uselessness and incompetency emanating from Gene's own family-of-origin experience. The couple began to bicker frequently, each partner blaming the other for their sorely felt unhappiness. Periods of antagonism and distance alternated with phases of enmeshment and infatuation.

In therapy, sessions were conducted with the couple together as well as for each partner separately. The beginning work aimed at a toning down of the anger expressed by Gene and Bea. The couple were asked to recognize and appreciate that the anger was a signal, an expression that things were out of balance. However, a continuation of the belligerent mode of relating was going to be unproductive for problem resolution and would only lead to further escalation and entrenchment. With considerable coaching, both spouses were able to place their anger on the sidelines, turn toward one another and gradually express their underlying hurts in a non-blaming manner. They came to realize that each was equally vulnerable and that the externalization (projective identification) of unhappiness onto the other was a mechanism that allowed for escape from internal distress in the short run but ultimately did not repair deeper layers of impaired self-esteem. Themes centered around the experience of incompetence for Gene and anticipated abandonment for Bea. In addition, this couple courageously explored their tendency to "place the other on a pedestal" when not fighting and how this Idealization was another version of escape from full self-awareness that includes coming face-to face with emotional pain and incompleteness.

Treatment proceeded with many crises alternating with periods of quiescence. As personal disclosure of mutual vulnerability became easier, a lighter mood evolved along with much humor and a sense of greater caring. Along with the support of the therapist, the emotional responsiveness of this couple's support system fostered powerful waves of empathy that washed over the spouses and bathed them in warmth. It reinforced a sense of goodness in two individuals who had felt deeply injured via early trauma that had been re-triggered within their previously stormy marriage. Over time, Gene and Bea began to feel less vulnerable intrapsychically as they felt safer in sharing their hurts on the interpersonal plane. This marriage turned into an equal emotional partnership.

CONCLUSION

The importance of a couple reaching the stage of Acceptance cannot be emphasized too much. Within the genuine empathic attunement of the Acceptance stage, a couple can fully experience emotional security, safety and true mutuality. Armed with these ingredients, the work of individuation, a lifetime journey, can proceed while use of Projective Identification is diminished. As each partner grows and evolves, so does the relationship. If this process toward self-realization can be maintained, the children of such partners witness and internalize something that is very powerful and enhancing. There is no better gift that two people can bestow on the generations to come.

REFERENCES

Becker E. (1973). *The denial of death.* New York: The Free Press.

Bowen, M. (1 978). *Family therapy in clinical practice.* New York: Jason Aronson.

Carter, E.A., & McGoldrick, M. (1989). Overview: The changing family life cycle–A framework for family therapy. In E. A. Carter & M. McGoldrick (Eds.), *The changing family life cycle.* Boston: Allyn & Bacon.

Erikson, E.H. (1950). *Childhood and society.* New York: W.W. Norton.

Erikson, E. H. (1979). *Identity and the life cycle.* New York: W. W. Norton.

Gottman, J.M. (1994). *What predicts divorce? The relationship between marital processes and marital outcomes.* Hillsdale, New Jersey: Lawrence Erlbaum Publishers.

Gordon, L. (1990). *Love knots.* New York: DellPublishers.

Grotstein, J.S. (1981). *Splitting and projective identification.* New York: Jason Aronson.

Haley, J. (1980). *Leaving home.* NewYork: McGraw-Hill.

Hetherington, E.M., Law, T.C., & O'Connor, T. G. (1993). Divorce: Challenges, changes, and new chances. In F. Walsh (Ed.), *Normal Family Processes* (2nd Edition). New York: Guilford.

Jacobson, N. & Christensen, A. (1996). *Integrative couple therapy.* New York: W.W. Norton.

Klein, M. (1946). Some notes on the schizoid mechanisms. *International Journal of Psychoanalysis, 27,* 99-110.

Kissen, M. (1996). Projective identification in couples. *American Journal of Psychotherapy, 50, 1,* 54-65.

McAdams, D.P. (1989). *Intimacy: The need to be close.* New York: Doubleday.

Markman, H., Stanley, S. & Blumberg, S. (1996). *Fighting for your marriage.* San Francisco: Jossey-Bass.

Mones, A.G. & Panitz, P.E. (1994). Marital violence: An integrated systems approach. *Journal of Social Distress and the Homeless, 3,* 39-51.

Nadelson, C.C., Polonsky, D.C., & Mathews, M.A. (1984). Marriage as developmental process. In C.C. Nadelson & D.C. Polonsky (Eds.), *Marriage and divorce: A contemporary perspective.* New York: Guilford.

Patalano, F. (1997). Developing the working alliance in marital therapy: A psychodynamic perspective. *Contemporary Family Therapy, 19,* 497-505.

Peck, J.S. & Manocherian, J. (1989). Divorce in the changing family life cycle. In E.A. Carter & M. McGoldrick (Eds.), *The changing family life cycle.* Boston: Allyn and Bacon.

Scarf, M. (1987). *Intimate partners: Patterns in love and marriage.* New York: Ballantine.

Scharff, D. & Scharff, J. (1991). *Object relations couple therapy.* New York: Jason Aronson.

Scharff, J. (1992). *Projective and introjective identification and the use of the therapist's self.* New York: Jason Aronson.

Schnarch, D.M. (1991). *Constructing the family crucible: An integration of sexual and marital therapy.* New York: W.W. Norton.

Schwartz, R.C. (1995). *Internal family systems therapy.* New York: Guilford.

Siegel, J. (1991). Analysis of projective identification: An object-relations approach to marital treatment. *Clinical Social Work Journal, 19, 1,* 71-81.

Walker, L.E. (1991). Post-traumatic stress disorder in women: Diagnosis and treatment of battered woman syndrome. *Psychotherapy, 28,* 1, 21-29.

Destiny or Illusion: The Impact of Family-of-Origin Patterns Among Pre-Marital Couples

Patrick J. Morrissette

SUMMARY. The potential influence of problematic family-of-origin patterns varies in degree and significance among pre-marital couples. Having witnessed the effects of family conflict or irresponsible parental behavior during their formative years as children, either or both partners become dispirited and feel trapped in a perceived intergenerational process destined to fail. This paper discusses clinical intervention with couples who are considering first time marriage and who report fear regarding the infiltration and eventual emergence of dysfunctional family-of-origin patterns within their own relationship. A three phase treatment program that involves disclosing fears of destiny, the promotion of skepticism, and relationship maintenance is outlined, discussed, and augmented by case vignettes. *[Article copies available for a fee from The Haworth Document Delivery Service: 1-800-342-9678. E-mail address: <getinfo@haworthpressinc.com> Website: <http://www.HaworthPress.com>]*

KEYWORDS. Pre-marital, intergenerational, family-of-origin

A segment of clinical couples who seek pre-marital counseling express a concern and reservation about the future of their relationship due to

---

Patrick J. Morrissette, PhD, is Associate Professor, School of Health Studies, Brandon University.

Address correspondence to: Patrick J. Morrissette, 270-18th Street, Brandon, Manitoba, Canada, R7A 6A9.

[Haworth co-indexing entry note]: "Destiny or Illusion: The Impact of Family-of-Origin Patterns Among Pre-Marital Couples." Morrissette, Patrick J. Co-published simultaneously in *Journal of Couples Therapy* (The Haworth Press, Inc.) Vol. 9, No. 1/2, 2000, pp. 67-84; and: *Couples Connecting: Prerequisites of Intimacy* (ed: Barbara Jo Brothers) The Haworth Press, Inc., 2000, pp. 67-84. Single or multiple copies of this article are available for a fee from The Haworth Document Delivery Service [1-800-342-9678, 9:00 a.m. - 5:00 p.m. (EST). E-mail address: getinfo@haworthpressinc.com].

problematic family-of-origin (FOO) behaviors and patterns. This clinical population can be contrasted with couples who perceive themselves as beyond the influence of their FOO's and underestimate how FOO's can influence mate selection and relationship functioning (Giblin, 1994). Although both partners within the former group may be apprehensive about the quality and longevity of their relationship, this apprehension is usually manifest in one partner. Rarely however, does this issue remain isolated within one partner thus effecting the couple dyad.

As a result of their anxiety, couples find themselves confused and begin to wonder whether they should pursue or terminate a relationship which is gratifying and promising. When queried about their dilemma, they describe a fear that dysfunctional behaviors and patterns which were evident in their FOO's will begin to slowly infiltrate their intimate relationship. A perceived logical solution, which is shared by many couples, is postponing marriage until they are certain that their relationship has eluded the grip of problematic patterns. This waiting period, however, can be long lasting and laden with unwarranted worry. Hoffman and Rosman (1990) indicate that marital phobia can be accompanied by symptoms that include chest pains, sweating, and shortness of breath.

Although reporting satisfaction during the early phases of the courtship period, some couples become disenchanted after minor disagreements and arguments. During the reconciliation process one or both partners recount how their parents entered into similar disputes and how emotional and/or physical violence inevitably ensued. At this point, couples begin to question their skills as a result of the modeling they witnessed as children and adolescents. When reflecting on past experiences, they conclude that it is unlikely that they have the ability to alter this trend. In their estimation, it is critical that youngsters witness respect, kindness, and love between parents to succeed in an intimate relationship. In short, these individuals perceive themselves as permanently scarred and doubtful about avoiding dysfunctional behavior in their own relationship. To assist pre marital couples during the deliberation process, this paper discusses a three phase treatment program that explores, challenges, and dispels family-of-origin concerns.

PRE-MARITAL PROGRAMS: AN OVERVIEW

A variety of pre-marital instruments (e.g., Giblin, 1994; Fowers, Montel, & Olson, 1996; Larsen & Olson, 1989), prevention programs (e.g., Boisvert, LaDoucer, Beaudry, & Freeston, 1995; Floyd, Markman, Kelly, Blumberg, & Stanley, 1995; Parrish, 1992; Shiloh, Reznik, Mariassa, & Boleslav, 1995; Wright, 1990), and education programs (e.g., Senediak, 1990) are available to assist professionals and couples identify areas of potential concern. Several authors (e.g., Giblin, 1994; Verdoff, Douvan, & Hatchett, 1995; Wood & Stroup, 1990) remark that historically, the helping and pastoral professions have been involved in pre-marital counseling to screen people who are clearly mismatched and to avoid eventual separation and divorce. Results from longitudinal studies, however, question the effectiveness of pre-marital programs in terms of better marital outcomes, increased participation of at-risk couples, and the improved effectiveness of these programs in community settings (e.g., Sullivan & Bradbury, 1997). Along the same lines, Williams (1992) noted a need for research to prove the effectiveness of pre-marital preparation. It is important for example, to determine what types of pre-marital programs are most effective with different types of couples preparing for marriage. Interestingly, Verdoff, Douvan, and Hatchett (1995) report that most modern couples do not participate in pre-marital reflection and evaluation despite the apparent need to do so considering the important decision of marriage.

THE IMPACT OF FAMILY-OF-ORIGIN ON INTIMATE RELATIONSHIPS

Attention rendered to the impact of FOO's on intimate relationships has typically been generated by intergenerational family theorists and practitioners (e.g., Giblin, 1994; Wood & Stroup, 1990). A key element in Bowen systems theory as it relates to couple dynamics, for example, pertains to fusion and the differentiation of self (Aylmer, 1986). Inherent in this process is the issue of emotional maturity and an examination of how personal values differ from one's FOO. Although theory pertaining to FOO's and intimate relationships is available, empirical research regarding the relationship between FOO's and intimate relationships is scant. An exception is a study conducted by Verdoff, Douvan, and Hatchett (1995) who report that although there exist some research available on the aspect of women's family experience, the same is not true for men. A variety of theories exist pertaining to the family transmission of marital instability among women and are based on (a) lower economic status of families-of-origin, (b) role-modeling, (c) poor socialization skills. Verdoff, Douvan, and Hatchett (1995) elaborate on pre-marital factors that include: social status of the partners (e.g., parents education, personal education, personal income, race), their family backgrounds (e.g., broken home, number of siblings, presence of older siblings), and their own pre-marital history as a couple (e.g., co-habitation, pre-marital pregnancy, length of courtship). According to these authors, these factors also interact with the personality and personal factors of each partner (e.g., power orientation, ambitiousness, cooperativeness, religion) and serve as antecedents to what can transpire in a marriage. They also suggest that the impact of the structure of FOO's may be instrumental in the understanding of marital instability.

REINFORCING FACTORS

Significant others can greatly influence how couples perceive their relationship and behave toward one another. Couples who are in regular contact with their FOO's, for example, tend to report hearing about or witnessing the very patterns they dread. Such patterns reinforce their pessimistic outlook and diminish any chance of a successful marriage. During an initial interview, one partner expressed how she was beginning to behave like her mother which was something she vowed she would not do. When questioned further, she explained that during arguments she would withdraw from the conflict and would refuse to speak to her partner for several days. When reflecting on this behavior, she recalled her mother behaving in a similar fashion and eventually divorcing her father after what seemed to be years of grief. As the client described her apprehension, it became apparent that she was worried about having inherited this avoidance behavior and life script. In some ways, she perceived her behavior to be a genetic disposition which would prevent her from enjoying a loving and lasting relationship. Barth (1993) discusses this life script scenario in the context of family illness and writes, "The legacy of family illness sometimes convinces them that nothing they do can overcome the inevitability of getting the illness and dying from it at a time preordained by family *history* [italics original], no matter how early in life. They are doomed" (p. xi). It is not unusual for such a life script to be transposed to an intimate relationship.

Parents who have experienced a dissatisfying relationship can greatly influence their adult child's decision making process. Re-living stories of mistreatment and despondency serve to further warn offspring about the potential risks associated with intimate relationships. Such disclosures seem especially frequent with parents who have not resolved their own issues and continually bring unfinished business into the present. This scenario was clearly illustrated in one case that involved a male client's father who arrived home after work one day only to find that his wife had decided to leave him for another man. Feeling betrayed and exploited, the client's father regularly berated women, warned of their deception, and encouraged his son's cynicism regarding intimate relationships.

Although a number of theories exist regarding why a parent would highlight such experiences (e.g., well-intended protectiveness), the potential impact of this behavior on adult children cannot be dismissed. A form of enmeshment appears in these parent-adult child relationships wherein parents reinforce the notion that their offspring are unable to separate and establish their own distinctive life. Inherent in these interactions is the implicit message that there is a loss of freedom. An obvious problem with such parent-adult child relationships is that offspring are without parents in whom to confide and seek direction. A common remark made by parents who remain wounded by unfinished business is that intimate partners are basically alike and untrustworthy.

From the outset it should be made clear that, in the author's opinion, such clients are not using historical family patterns as a convenient way to terminate a relationship, although this may be true in some situations. Rather, these individuals are seeking therapy to confirm or refute their worries. The challenge in assisting young, impressionable couples however, increases when faulty/allegory-based thought patterns are reinforced by significant others.

SIBLING STORIES

Amplification of fatalistic beliefs can occur when clients witness siblings who appear to have replicated problematic behaviors, are struggling in their relationships, or have experienced a failed relationship. These circumstances tend to provide evidence and serve to reinforce their theory of doom. To avoid becoming another casualty, clients work toward establishing a safe emotional distance and begin to withdraw from their intimate relationships. On a rational level, clients understand that their relationships are distinct from their siblings. Nevertheless, they remain haunted by what they consider to be a biological thread that connects them and dictates their behavior.

CASE VIGNETTE

Jim and Carol sought therapy to improve their communication. Early in therapy it was revealed that Jim enjoyed a very close relationship with his older brother. Jim described his brother as a friend and trusted confidant. While discussing his difficulty in sharing intimate information with Carol, Jim intimated that he was warned by his brother to avoid personal disclosure because it could result in a high sense of vulnerability and loss of power in a relationship. To no surprise, Jim's brother remained emotionally distraught as a result of a failed relationship with a woman to whom he was engaged. In many ways, Jim was being coached into a self-protective mode. Although Jim could not provide evidence why he could not safely share intimate information with Carol, he was hesitant to do so and enjoy a trusting relationship. Consequently, the lack of expressed trust between Jim and Carol threatened their relationship and future together.

LACK OF INVESTMENT IN THE RELATIONSHIP

A problem encountered by pre-marital couples during the deliberation process is the increasing lack of emotional investment and intimacy. In some ways, couples experience stagnation and are hesitant to invest in their relationship. Perceiving their relationship as destined for failure, they enter into a self-protective mode and become hypervigilant about possible exploitation and unnecessary emotional distress. This appears to be particularly true with clients who perceived a parent as a victim of spousal exploitation. In these cases, clients remain guarded in an effort to ensure that boundaries and personal rights are not transgressed. Associating a partner with a parent who was perceived as exploitative is a common occurrence and results in statements such as: *I won't let you do to me what my father did to my mother* [italics added] or *You're just like my mother* [italics added]. Such statements can be verbalized or remain a part of a client's cognitive schema. Clearly, these statements provide invaluable information about client history and personal trepidation. Foster (1993) elaborates on this issue and states:

> Problems repeat in patterns because people are likely to do what is familiar, even when it is clearly not working. Because it's familiar, you don't realize that there is another possible course of action. The root of your old ways of doing things goes back to your family experiences from childhood and adolescence. If you back track through the development of a problem, you will come to the roots of it in your early family life. (p. 22)

CASE VIGNETTE

During their initial interview involving Susan and Barbara, the couple described how, over a period of time, Susan became hypervigilant and very territorial. For example, she began to bake for herself and would clearly separate her food from Barbara's. This particular issue was especially important and meaningful for Barbara, who was from a family where food was always shared and a symbol of intimacy. Consequently, Barbara perceived Susan's separation of food as a deeper and personally troubling metaphor. Rather than process her emotional pain with Susan, Barbara began to slowly withdraw and found herself becoming interested in another woman at work.

INTERRUPTING THE CYCLE

The idea of interrupting a dysfunctional intergenerational cycle can be appealing to many couples. Despite appearing resigned to the notion that their relationship is doomed, the very fact that couples initiate therapy suggests that they are defiant and reluctant to surrender their future without a fight. Inherent in their behavior is a willingness to defy the odds while forging a new path. Punctuating the fact that these couples have considered therapy, organized their lives to attend treatment, and have begun to take control of their own relationship by challenging the odds can be revealing and empowering. During this process, the inherent strengths and coping mechanisms of the couple become more obvious.

A concern for the welfare of children is also evidenced by many couples who are in the deliberation process of maintaining or terminating their intimate relationship. Having been exposed to an unhappy childhood themselves, these couples want to avoid subjecting children to the sadness they had to endure as a result of parental disputes, disharmony, and divorce. What becomes obvious about these couples is their insight and protectiveness. In the author's experience, couples take these personal characteristics for granted and fail to see how these personal traits are fundamentally critical to responsible child rearing practices. At such points during treatment, major distinctions can be drawn for couples to distinguish them from their FOO's. When asked to contrast their perspectives about responsible child rearing practices with their personal experiences, couples begin to identify and comment on differences between the generations. When a distinction is drawn, what inevitably strikes them is their concern for children and the attention they have unknowingly rendered to their relationship. Following this distinction, a line of questioning can follow regarding how couples are able to reassess and formulate their own path, both in terms of child-rearing practices and relationship building.

STAGES OF TREATMENT

Although a straightforward clinical approach that underscores personal agency might be effective in addressing such problems, client couples who are entrenched in believing that family patterns are impossible to change, may require additional effort and action-oriented strategies. The latter approach, goes beyond analytical talk and invites clients to create the very situations which have effectively frightened and controlled them. In essence, couples experience tangible events which are considered more meaningful. Three distinct stages of treatment including disclosing fears of destiny, promotion of skepticism, and relationship maintenance are discussed below.

DISCLOSING FEARS OF DESTINY

Initially couples are reluctant to disclose their anxiety fearing that their concerns will not be taken seriously by therapists and prematurely dismissed. Some couples report on previous clinical experiences where their concerns were considered irrational or simply an overreaction thus, contributing to their premature withdrawal from treatment. When working with this clinical population, initial contact is particularly important. Moreover, it is critical that their problem not be trivialized and glossed over. Suggesting, for example, that things usually blow over, or that they are merely experiencing the symptoms of cold feet, misses the mark and can jeopardize the therapeutic relationship. Couples who feel misunderstood will likely withdraw from treatment and continue along their current course. Consequently, the engagement phase of treatment is very important and must provide couples with an opportunity to tell their story, share their fears, and hear each other's concerns (Egan, 1994). This is important because couples tend to apologize for taking up valuable clinical time with an issue that appears to pale in contrast to other clinical problems.

The engagement phase is also an ideal time to begin highlighting a couple's insight and commitment to one another. It can be pointed out that, rather than following a trail of doom, the couple is being proactive and is combining forces to maintain their relationship. A critical question that couples can be asked during this phase relates to how they have managed to remain together and invested in their relationship. Rather than resigning themselves to the fact that their relationship is destined for failure, what can be underscored is a couple's resiliency and determination.

PROMOTION OF SKEPTICISM

The second phase of treatment replicates a de-programming process whereby a context is co-created with couples to gradually identify, explore, and challenge long standing beliefs and the meanings attributed to these beliefs (Byng-Hall, 1995). During this phase of treatment, couples are encouraged to investigate and experiment while engaging in potentially playful activities. The purpose of this phase is to have couples identify and gather FOO data which is perceived as threatening to their relationship and overall happiness (e.g., excessive drinking, name calling during arguments, threats to abandon the relationship). After some data have been collected, couples are invited to purposefully place themselves in situations where such behaviors generally occur in their own lives. The idea of producing situations that are associated with intensity and strife may be intimidating for couples and the antithesis of what they were expecting. Although they realize that avoiding situations that are potentially conflicting has not strengthened their relationship, avoiding contentious issues seems logical and safe. One or both partners may believe that if a problem situation is manufactured, things may become uncontrollable and result in increased distress and irreparable damage. Inherent in this thinking is the couple's lack of confidence in controlling and managing their emotions and behavior. They may believe that a locus of control is externally rather than internally determined.

Taking charge of their relationship, and creating a new life script, generally means going in direct opposition to established FOO behavioral and interactional styles. In essence, this process involves breaking the FOO trance (Bradshaw, 1988). As noted by Foster (1993), accomplishing this task may be more challenging than first anticipated because repeating family patterns can provide a sense of belonging and security and are basically convenient and comforting. Suggesting that couples move out of their comfort zone and psychological root system (Foster, 1993) and into unknown territory can trigger a sense of apprehension. During this process, implanted beliefs will be questioned while a powerful pull from FOO influence is simultaneously experienced. The level of stress associated with a sense of divided loyalties between self and FOO can emotionally paralyze clients and obstruct their growth and therefore, should not be underestimated. The amount of time devoted to this stage will be unique to each couple and will be dictated by their circumstances.

What is often detected at this point in therapy is the couples' extreme sensitivity to normal conflicts within an intimate relationship and a concern that there will be a loss of control. To assist couples in generating useful data, while dispelling erroneous beliefs about their relationship, they can be invited to participate in out-of-session pretend tasks (Hoffman & Rosman, 1990; Madanes, 1981) that may include disagreements. In other words, couples are encouraged to experience the very situations they fear, albeit in a playful way. In elaborating on the pretend strategy, Madanes (1981) writes:

> The directive to pretend to have the symptom is less limiting and restrictive than is the directive to actually have the symptom. It provides the opportunity to respond in less structured ways. The response to the paradoxical directive to actually have the symptom is either to have it or not have it. The response to the directive to pretend to have the symptom is more unpredictable but also more creative and spontaneous. (p. 73)

This strategy also indirectly reflects the therapist's faith in a couple's ability to ward off unwanted patterns, effectively resolve their differences, and enjoy a harmonious relationship. Opposed to encouraging couples to avoid problematic issues, therapists deliberately refuse to give unwarranted power to irritating problems or patterns. Byng-Hall (1995) notes that while clients are engaged in the exploration phase, therapists can also become temporary attachment figures and provide a temporary security base from which couples can search for solutions. Hoffman and Rosman (1990) remark that pretending exercises enable clients to expose themselves to fears without the accompanying overwhelming anxieties. Furthermore, clients can increase their self confidence, control their fears and environment and can become interested in further experimentation. Essentially, couples and therapists collude to defeat problematic patterns and fortify the therapeutic relationship.

CASE VIGNETTE

During the assessment interview, Brian and Mary discussed how they were unable to make a mutual purchase without having the event turn into a full blown argument. This concerned them because in their opinion, a marriage usually entailed the joint purchase of various items. It seemed that this couple was entering into a self-fulfilling prophecy before even entering a store. Their anxiety about an inevitable fight created enormous stress for both partners and shopping trips typically resulted in each partner threatening a boycott of future joint purchases. Although this strategy can be a very practical solution to such a presenting problem, it was clear that this was not the solution for which the couple was searching. In an effort to help the couple gather valuable information about the skills necessary to ward off patterns, they were invited to initiate pretend disagreements and conflicts. The couple was assigned the additional task of not resolving the issue but to simply gather information about precipitating events, personal behaviors and reactions, and partner responses. In short, the couple was encouraged to invite old patterns as an indirect way to control their relationship.

Upon their return for the second interview a week later, Brian and Mary reported some interesting findings. For example, Mary disclosed how she purposefully tried to instigate an argument by instructing Brian how to drive on the way to the mall. In Mary's mind, although not discussed in therapy, this behavior (giving directions) was an ongoing source of conflict in the relationship. To Mary's surprise however, Brian did not become upset as he normally did but rather became amused with Mary's attempt at fulfilling the out-of-session task. The playfulness that resulted from their interaction in the car flowed over into their shopping trip and apparently contributed to an enjoyable and less stressful evening together. In addition to becoming more sensitive to habits that threatened their relationship, Brian and Mary became more aware of their commitment to each other.

The purpose of pretend tasks is to have couples experience control over the behaviors which they have come to fear. Once they begin realizing that their fate is in their hands, and not dictated by history, they enter into a state of skepticism. As such, they have the opportunity to challenge various myths to which they had formerly succumbed. It is this skepticism which frees them up to consider alternatives and create a different belief system. At this point, the notion of relinquishing one's power of choice, while assuming a victim role, can be introduced and pursued. Introducing such notions can create a degree of cognitive dissonance for couples and help them begin to entertain alternate perceptions of the problem. In essence, couples are placed in a position wherein cognitive space is created and alternative perspectives can be entertained.

RELATIONSHIP MAINTENANCE

Maintaining a healthy and gratifying relationship becomes a critical and ongoing stage for couples. This may be especially true in cases where the history between couples has been brief or troubled. In short, time to gain experience and establish elements of trust and confidence is required.

The maintenance of a relationship basically involves a continual two step process. First, couples are encouraged to remain aware of behaviors and patterns which threaten the vitality of their relationship. For example, one couple created a visual cue in the form of a checklist of relationship-threatening behaviors which could invade and hinder their relationship (e.g., lack of personal time together, snide remarks). Both partners posted their lists on their refrigerators. Furthermore, to remain vigilant of such insidious behaviors and patterns, both partners shared lists and collaborated to keep their relationship free of these unwanted trends. A natural spin-off of this creative approach is that couples form an alliance and supportive approach to problem solving. Perhaps more importantly, couples realize the daily effort involved in maintaining their relationship. To them, relationship maintenance was not a magical process that occurred naturally but rather a process that required work and ongoing attention.

Second, behaviors which nourish and strengthen relationships are advocated. This strategy was used by another couple who made a point of selecting and enjoying activities that served to bring them closer together. Such exercises rarely involve the expenditure of money and require that couples spend time together. Long walks and intimate talks, for example, are very popular. According to Giblin (1994) contentious areas within an intimate relationship may become less toxic through discussion and negotiation. This former process provides the opportunity for partners to gain insight into themselves and each other. Although initially appearing straightforward, this process is multifaceted and involves identifying, negotiating, planning, and participation. Although couples are generally efficient in the first three facets of this particular process, actually earmarking time to complete a planned activity becomes the greatest challenge. Many couples comment on the unexpected distractions they encounter and the importance of prioritizing their relationship. To do so, couples need to establish safeguards (e.g., disconnecting the telephone during intimate conversations, spending quality time alone) to protect their time together.

To further enhance and solidify relationships, some couples agree to participate in on-going relationship education sessions. This proactive approach provides couples with the opportunity to meet with therapists to review their short and long term goals and progress. These sessions are framed as *relationship fitness* [italics added] consultation sessions and are designed to underscore their strengths. An analogy to physical fitness training is drawn to help couples better appreciate the need for continual strength building exercises. The scheduling of relationship fitness consultation sessions will obviously vary with couple needs.

CASE VIGNETTE

To test their commitment to one another, Bill and Karen decided to attend a family gathering where excessive drinking was the norm and where embarrassing disputes among partners was common. Prior to this experiment the couple had avoided family gatherings fearing that Bill would fall prey to this irresponsible behavior. Bill had shared childhood incidences with Karen whereby his father would become intoxicated at various family events and behave irresponsibly. After careful deliberation, the couple agreed to test the water, attend a family function, and enjoy a social drink as they often did together when away from their FOO's.

Prior to the family function, the couple was advised to independently list problematic behaviors but not share this information with each other. Rather, the couple was advised to exchange their notes mid-way through the family function as a review process. Although apprehensive, the couple remained committed to attending the family function and agreed to the therapeutic task.

When queried about the evening during a follow-up interview, the couple described their anticipation regarding the content of their respective lists. To their relief however, each list contained similar concerns (e.g., being swayed by group pressure, feeling agitated and irritable). In addition, the couple was surprised by the number of times they were invited to drink excessively and *join the party* [italics added]. In essence, the couple discovered something about their own boundaries and more importantly, their ability to maintain limits and respect for one another. Although only a small step, the couple considered the exercise useful, revealing, and a confidence builder. In short, the experience punctuated behaviors that were essential to their happiness.

According to the couple, they learned valuable information about themselves and one another. For example, during the evening Karen noticed and admired Bill's ability to politely decline offers to drink excessively. She perceived this behavior as indicative of maturity, self-control, and respect for her. On the other hand, Bill appreciated Karen's confidence in him by not monitoring his alcohol consumption or continually expressing her fear of excessive drinking during the evening. Furthermore, the couple realized the importance of protecting their time together. Overall, the couple reported an increased sense of security in their relationship.

THE ISSUE OF RELAPSE

It is not unusual for couples to become alarmed when a period of progress is followed by a major disagreement or when it appears that problematic patterns are re-appearing. Generally, their immediate reaction is that they have been unsuccessful in warding off such patterns. Knowing that couples will likely slip into old ways of behaving, understanding and predicting relapse can be very useful. Johnson (1995) writes:

> Since variations in behavior are natural and normal, it is also natural for patients to have lapses back to previous forms of behavior. If the therapist can predict and discuss this ahead of time, it motivates the patient to continue in the good behavior despite relapses. By discussing the relapse, the therapist normalizes it as a variation which is to be expected, even learned from. But if the therapist were to avoid discussing relapse, the patient might interpret a slip as a catastrophe and give up any effective coping. (p. 153)

Johnson (1995) highlights various strategies that can be utilized to assist couples in surviving setbacks and includes (a) predicting the relapse, (b) advocating the relapse, and (c) rehearsing the relapse and recovery in fantasy. In discussing relapse openly, couple are placed in a position of authority and control. Rather than anxiously awaiting for relapse to occur, couples dictate and arrange when problematic patterns can occur. Couples begin to realize that minor setbacks can be anticipated in any relationship and their emergence does not signify disaster. For example, it can be explained to couples that undesirable patterns generally rear their ugly heads when it is least expected. Therefore, it becomes important for couples to remain sensitive to antecedent events that typically contribute to disputes. Within this clinical intervention, couples are invited to remain closely allied against forces that can negatively effect their relationship.

A creative example of how couples can be invited to externalize problems and regain a sense of personal agency in their relationship is demonstrated in the work of White (White & Epston, 1990). White presents a way of helping clients combine forces against unwanted patterns rather than each other. The externalization of problems is described as:

> . . . an approach to therapy that encourages persons to objectively and, at times, to personify the problems that they experience as oppressive. In this process, the problem becomes a separate entity

> and thus external to the person or relationship that was ascribed as the problem. Those problems that are considered to be inherent, as well as those relatively fixed qualities that are attributed to persons and to relationships, are rendered less fixed and less restricting. (White & Epston, 1990, p. 38)

The externalization of problems is particularly appealing to couples because a new sense of personal agency can be fostered and they are able to assume responsibility for exploring different choices and possibilities.

THE ROLE OF PERSONAL THERAPY

Although much of the work described here takes place in the context of couples therapy, there may be instances where individual work with one partner is requested or indicated. Some partners may need additional encouragement and support during the therapeutic process. In the author's experience, the partner who requests individual therapy is worried about contaminating and destroying the relationship. At this point, a coaching role can be assumed by therapists. In other words, therapists play an active role by continuing to motivate the client while down playing old thought patterns that may seep through and contribute to client uncertainty.

When individual therapy is agreed upon by therapists and couples, the focus of treatment needs to remain systemic in nature and any subtle attempts to criticize absent partners should be discouraged. Obviously, therapists need to be particularly sensitive to their position within the therapeutic triangle and wisely establish and clarify their policy regarding the disclosure of confidential information during individual sessions. Assisting couples during their deliberation process is rarely an easy endeavor and can involve intense moments. To avoid unnecessary misunderstandings and conflict, it is essential that the focus of individual treatment not drift to the absent partner. Some couples have found it useful to have individual sessions either video or audio taped for an absent partner. These tapes can alleviate unwarranted concerns and provide absent partners with a new window into their partner's life and experience.

CONCLUSION

The fear and weight of dysfunctional FOO patterns and behaviors can effectively stymie a couple's relationship and future plans. As a way of countering pessimistic predictions and unfortunate historical trends, a three phase treatment plan is suggested whereby couples join forces in a collaborative effort to defeat the odds and forge their own future. As discussed in this paper, the initial engagement phase of therapy is especially important since clinical couples who present with this concern may be perceived as over-reactive and consequently, feel misunderstood.

During the course of treatment, therapists can play an instrumental role by punctuating couples' strength and commitment to their relationship. To help couples identify and experience success, especially when facing critical situations, playful out-of-session tasks are assigned and behavioral results are monitored by couples.

REFERENCES

Aylmer, R. (1986). Bowen family systems marital therapy. In N. S. Jacobson and A. S. Gurman (Eds.). *Clinical handbook of marital therapy* (pp. 107-148). New York: Guilford.

Barth, J. (1993). *It runs in my family: Overcoming the legacy of family illness.* New York: Brunner/Mazel.

Boisvert, J., LaDoucer, R., Beaudry, M., & Freeston, M. (1995). Perception of marital problems and of their prevention by Quebec young adults. *Journal of Genetic Psychology, 156,* 33-44.

Byng-Hall, J. (1995). *Re-writing family scripts: Improvisation and systems change.* New York: Guilford.

Bradshaw, J. (1988). *Bradshaw on: The Family.* Florida: Health Communications.

Egan, G. (1994). *The skilled helper: A problem-management approach to helping* (5th ed.). Pacific Grove, CA: Brooks/Cole.

Floyd, F., Markman, H., Kelly, S., Blumberg, S., & Stanley, S. (1995). Preventive intervention and relationship enhancement. In N. S. Jacobson & A. S. Gurman (Eds.), *Clinical handbook of couple therapy* (pp. 212-230). New York: Guilford.

Foster, C. (1993). *The family patterns workbook: Breaking free from your past and creating a life of your own.* New York: Tarcher/Perigee.

Fowers, B., Montel, K., & Olson, D. (1996). Predicting marital success for pre-marital couple types based on PREPARE. *Journal of Marital and Family Therapy, 22,* 103-119.

Giblin, P. (1994). Premarital preparation: Three approaches. *Pastoral Psychology, 42,* 147-161.

Hoffman, S., & Rosman, L. (1990). Strategic approaches to "marital phobia": A case study. *Family Therapy, 2,* 157-162.

Johnson, L. (1995). *Psychotherapy in the age of accountability.* New York: Norton.

Larsen, A., & Olson, D. (1989). Predicting marital satisfaction using PREPARE: A replication study. *Journal of Marital and Family Therapy, 15,* 311-322.

Madanes, C. (1981). *Strategic family therapy.* California: Jossey-Bass.

Parrish, E. (1992). A quasi-experimental evaluation of the pre-marital assessment program for pre-marital counselling. *Australian and New Zealand Journal of Family Therapy, 13,* 33-336.

Senediak, C. (1990). The value of pre-marital education. *Australian and New Zealand Journal of Family Therapy, 11,* 26-31.

Shiloh, S., Reznik,, H., Mariassa, B., & Boleslav, G. (1995). Pre-marital genetic counselling to consanguineous couples. Attitudes and beliefs and decisions among counselled, non-counselled and unrelated couples in Israel. *Social Sciences Medicine, 41,* 1301-1310.

Sullivan, K., & Bradbury, T. (1997). Are pre-marital programs reaching couples at risk for marital dysfunction? *Journal of Consulting and Counseling Psychology, 65,* 24-30.

Verdoff, J., Douvan, E., & Hatchett, S. (1995). *Marital instability: A social and behavioral study of the early years.* Connecticut: Praeger.

White, M. & Epston, D. (1990). *Narrative means to a therapeutic end.* New York: Norton.

Williams, L. (1992). Premarital counseling: A needs assessment among engaged individuals. *Contemporary Family Therapy, 14,* 505-518.

Wood, N. & Stroup, H. (1990). Family systems in premarital counseling. *Pastoral Psychology, 39,* 111-119.

Wright, J. (1990). Getting engaged: A case study and a model of the engagement period as a process of conflict resolution. *Counseling Psychology Quarterly, 3,* 399-408.

A Typology of Anger Profiles in Couples

Kathleen Laughrea
John Wright
Pierre McDuff
Claude Bélanger

SUMMARY. Few researchers have attempted to identify couples' anger management profiles. Cluster analysis was conducted using five indices of anger derived from Inventory of Anger Experience in Couples (Laughrea, Bélanger, & Wright, 1996). Sample consisted of 220 couples from normal and clinical populations. Four types were identified: (a) Re-

Kathleen Laughrea, PhD, is Assistant Professor, Department of Psychology, University of Moncton.

John Wright, PhD, is Titular Professor, and Pierre McDuff, MSc, is Research Associate, Department of Psychology, University of Montreal.

Claude Bélanger, PhD, is Assistant Professor, Department of Psychology, University of Quebec at Montreal.

Address correspondence to: Kathleen Laughrea, Department of Psychology, University of Moncton, Moncton, New-Brunswick, Canada, E1A 3E9, or to John Wright, Department of Psychology, University of Montreal, C.P. 6128, succ. Centre-ville, Montreal, Quebec, Canada, H3C 3J7. Electronic mail may be sent to Laughrk@umoncton.ca or to Wrightj@ere.umontreal.ca

The authors wish to express their appreciation to the clinical psychologists from the Clinique de consultation conjugale et familiale Poitras-Wright, Côté, in metropolitan Montreal, Quebec, Canada, for their participation in the data collection.

This research was supported in part by the fund FCAR (# 95ER1115) through a Quebec research grant to John Wright, Stéphane Sabourin, and Yvan Lussier. Kathleen Laughrea was supported by a doctoral fellowship from the fund FCAR, government of Quebec, and from CQRS, Ministry of health and social services, government of Quebec. This article was based on the doctoral dissertation of Kathleen Laughrea at University of Montreal.

[Haworth co-indexing entry note]: "A Typology of Anger Profiles in Couples." Laughrea, Kathleen et al. Co-published simultaneously in *Journal of Couples Therapy* (The Haworth Press, Inc.) Vol. 9, No. 1/2, 2000, pp. 85-107; and: *Couples Connecting: Prerequisites of Intimacy* (ed: Barbara Jo Brothers) The Haworth Press, Inc., 2000, pp. 85-107. Single or multiple copies of this article are available for a fee from The Haworth Document Delivery Service [1-800-342-9678, 9:00 a.m. - 5:00 p.m. (EST). E-mail address: getinfo@haworthpressinc.com].

laxed Couples, (b) Slightly Angry Couples, (c) Explosive Angry Couples, and (d) Dangerously Enraged Couples. Results also indicated that the higher the disturbance of anger dynamics between partners, the more psychologically and maritally distressed they were, and the lower the quality of their coping strategies. Understanding anger and its clinical implication are discussed. *[Article copies available for a fee from The Haworth Document Delivery Service: 1-800-342-9678. E-mail address: <getinfo@haworthpressinc.com> Website: <http://www.HaworthPress.com>]*

KEYWORDS. Anger, dyadic, cluster, coping, psychological distress

In the last fifteen years, many researchers have investigated the cognitive, affective, and behavioral markers that differentiate happy and unhappy marriages. It is now well-known that attribution processes and general thought patterns about negative behaviors have a considerable impact on partners' perceptions of their close relationships (Bradbury & Fincham, 1990; Karney & Bradbury, 1995; Laughrea, Bélanger, Sabourin, Lussier, & Wright, 1992). Many researchers have also underscored the importance of good communication skills in marital adjustment (Bélanger, Sabourin, & Wright, 1993; Boland & Follingstad, 1987; Krokoff, 1991). In addition, Gottman (1994), in a recent review of the relationship between marital interaction and marital satisfaction, underlined two different tendencies of satisfied and unsatisfied couples. First, distressed partners enhanced levels of negative affects and interaction, and they more often disagreed with, criticized, and showed verbal contempt for their partners. Second, distressed couples revealed difficulties in developing a positive acceptance attitude towards their partners and demonstrated different defensive behaviors. In managing their conflicts, they demonstrated worse coping strategies and problem solving skills than adapted couples did.

Some studies of dysfunctional couples dealing with conflict have emphasized a pattern of escalation, a pattern often marked by verbal attacks, which may be followed by physically abusive behavior (Murphy & O'Leary, 1989; O'Leary, Malone, & Tyree 1994; O'Leary & Vivian, 1990). The high psychological, social, and judicial costs of mismanaging conflicts have led some researchers to empirically evaluate the processes underlying conflict escalation between spouses and the relationship dynamics of violent couples.

To this end, Lloyd (1990) studied four groups of couples: nondistressed-nonviolent, nondistressed-violent, distressed-nonviolent, and distressed-violent. Results indicated that distressed-violent partners reported lower levels of problem solving skills and negotiation strategies, and were less likely to apologize after a conflict. They were also more likely than the other three groups to report verbal attacks and withdrawal patterns following heated arguments. Further elucidating the link between distress and violence, Lloyd (1990) found that although nondistressed-violent couples reported anger and verbal attack, they resolved their conflicts through negotiation more often than distressed-violent couples did. These results suggest that the relationship between conflict and violence appears to be mediated by the distress level of the marriage.

The work of Margolin and her colleagues is another good example of the study of the conflicts with violent couples (Burman, John, & Margolin, 1992; Burman, Margolin, & John, 1993; Margolin, John, & Gleberman, 1988; Margolin, John, & O'Brien, 1989). These researchers have used a behavioral-affective coding system to compare marital interaction between physically violent, verbally aggressive, withdrawing, and nondistressed couples. The findings highlight the role of negative interaction, anger, hostility, and nonconstructive approaches to conflict in physically violent marriages. This research group also found that nondistressed partners could occasionally improve conflicts, and could demonstrate negative reciprocity, hostile affect, and highly contingent behavior patterns like as verbally aggressive and withdrawing couples. The hallmark of these nondistressed couples, however, was their ability to end negative interaction cycles more quickly than the other groups (Burman et al., 1993). Along these lines, Markman (1991) had already postulated that all couples experience disagreements and conflicts and feel negative emotions such as anger, mistrust, fear, sadness, etc. The challenge for a couple is to handle these negative feelings constructively, so that a particular conflict does not lead to violence.

Among the negative emotions experienced in marriage, anger has received increasing attention, particularly in the context of marital violence (Burman et al., 1993; Jacobson, Gottman, Waltz, Rushe, Babcock, & Holtzworth-Munroe, 1994; Gottman, Jacobson, Rushe, Shortt, Babcock, La Taillade, & Waltz, 1995). Recently, Jacobson and his colleagues tried to discriminate between violent husbands with their wives and nonviolent but distressed couples on the basis of different negative affects in marital interaction. They separated the evaluation of anger, using an observational affect coding system, into three specific codes: anger (identified as a hostility dimension), contempt, and belligerence. These two last dimensions were characterized by an intense provocative anger code, which the researchers labeled an emotional aggression code. Results indicated that battering spouses were angrier than other couples and both were equally verbally aggressive towards each other. Only violent husbands could be discriminated from the other men on provocative codes, such as contempt and belligerence (Jacobson et al., 1994).

So far, few studies have specifically investigated, identified, and clarified the role of anger in marital adjustment. There is also an ongoing debate whether anger actually functions as a negative emotion in couples (Gottman 1994; Gottman & Krokoff, 1989). The present group of researchers recently explored this area by using a self-report measure based on Spielberger's (1988) theory. Spielberger's model suggests that a useful profile of how people manage their anger can be obtained using three anger dimensions: state anger, personality trait anger, and anger expression style. Since 1988, more than forty publications have emerged from Spielberger's anger measure, mostly in the fields of behavioral medicine, health, and social psychology. Our team has already translated the questionnaire into French and adapted it for the marital situation (Laughrea, Bélanger, & Wright, 1996). In previous research, we reported that one spouse's anger could strongly influence the other's. The intensity of state anger, modes of expression of anger, and the personality traits it reflects all affected the marital adjustment of each partner. Distressed couples also appeared to have more problems with their anger than nondistressed couples did (Laughrea, Bélanger, Wright, & McDuff, 1997).

Along these lines, this study proposed to understand better the escalation process in conflict management by identifying a typology of anger profiles within couples. It also attempted to clarify how the anger profiles of partners co-varied with dyadic adjustment, psychological distress, and marital coping skills. To our knowledge, scientific research on marriage has not explored the relationship dynamics of anger profiles within and across different couples, based on a self-report measure with Spielberger's approach. It was anticipated that different anger profiles between partners could be identified and that the quality of a couple's anger dynamics could also affect each partner's personal and marital adjustment. Further, it was predicted that the more dysfunctional a couple's anger profile, the more difficulty they would have managing their marital problems.

METHOD

Subjects

The sample consisted of 220 French-Canadian couples. Half were recruited from the community, half from a private marital and family clinic in metropolitan Montreal. To participate in this study, the spouses had to be between 25 years and 65 years old and had to have been living together for more than one year. The average length of marriage was 12 years (SD = 9.3). The mean number of children for the couples was 1.6 (SD = 1.1). Women's average age was 38 (SD = 8.6), with 15 years (SD = 2.9) of formal education. The majority of women were employed (80%); the mean annual income of all women was $26,000 Canadian ($SD$ = $12,500). The mean age for men was 40 (SD = 9.1), with an average formal education of 16 years (SD = 3.6). The majority were employed (91%), and the mean annual income of all men was $42,500 Canadian ($SD$ = $12,000).

Measures

Inventory of Anger Experience in Couples (IAEC), is a 32-item French version self-report (Laughrea et al., 1996) of the State-Trait Anger Expression Inventory (STAXI; Spielberger, 1988). The IAEC measures the experience and expression of anger in intimate relationships. The present researchers translated the original 44 items from the STAXI into French. Instructions and items are presented so that a person has to answer in terms of his or her anger towards the partner instead of a general mode of anger measured towards everybody, as in Spielberger's (1988) version.[1] Factor analysis, with all of the items or with the three parts separated (factor loadings = .30), indicated that 32 items are clearly sufficient to replicate Spielberger's theoretical model. Scoring is based on a Likert scale from 1 (almost never) to 4 (almost always).

The new version respected Spielberger's three-part questionnaire structure, using state anger (5 items), trait anger (8 items), and anger expression (19 items). The state anger scale measures the intensity of angry feelings, from mild irritation to intense fury and rage, towards the spouse at a particular time. The trait anger scale estimates an individual's disposition to perceive a wide range of situations as annoying or frustrating. The anger expression scale establishes three expression styles: anger-in (8 items), anger-out (3 items), and anger control (8 items). Anger-in measures how often angry feelings towards a partner were held in or suppressed; anger-out, how often an individual expresses anger, particularly in the form of sarcastic remarks, towards his or her spouse; and anger control, how often a partner attempts to control his or her expression of anger towards the spouse. Results of factor analysis and estimates of internal reliability revealed that French and English versions have similar psychometric properties. *Alpha*s ranged from .74 to .88 in the French version (Laughrea et al., 1996), and from .69 to .91 in the English version (Fuqua, Leonard, Masters, Smith, Campbell, & Fischer, 1991; Spielberger, 1988).

Since the French questionnaire contained fewer items than the English version, a standardized denominator was established for each scale; in this way, our scores could be compared with Spielberger's. In the current study, raw scores were calculated separately for each sex and were used to compare each others, whereas percentiles, using Spielberger's norms, were used to interpret couples' anger profiles and compare their anger dynamics. Spielberger (1988) suggested scale scores between the 25th and 75th percentiles could be considered in the normal range. The higher the score, the more a person is prone to experience intense anger. Spielberger recommended that scores above the 75th percentile be considered indicative of an anger profile that might interfere with optimal functioning. A person with such a profile might have difficulties in interpersonal relationships or develop psychological or physical disorders. Scores below the 25th percentile might indicate an underuse of one of the anger dimensions; low scores on all of the anger scales might indicate excessive use of denial and repression.

Dyadic Adjustment Scale (DAS) (Spanier, 1976) is a 32-item self-report questionnaire of marital adjustment. The DAS has been widely used in marital literature to assess couples' satisfaction with their marital relationship. The total score ranges from 0 to 151; the higher the score, the more a person feels satisfied with his or her intimate relationship. In concordance with previous research (Floyd & Markman, 1983), our study used 100 as a cutoff point dividing distressed and nondistressed spouses. This measure had reliability and discriminant validity in both French (*alphas* range from .61 to .91; Baillargeon, Dubois, & Marineau, 1986; Sabourin, Lussier, Laplante, & Wright, 1990) and English versions (*alphas* range from .72 to .85; Spanier, 1976; Spanier & Thompson, 1982).

Psychiatric Symptoms Index (PSI) (Ilfeld, 1976) is a brief version of the Hopkins Symptoms Checklist (Derogatis, Lipman, & Rickels, 1974). The PSI is a 29-item self-report measure of the presence of common psychiatric symptoms identified in the past week. Scoring is based on a Likert scale from 0 (not at all) to 3 (very often). Results of factor analysis indicated the presence of four syndromes: depression, anxiety, hostility, and cognitive disturbance (*alphas* range from .77 to .91; Ilfeld, 1976). Scores for each scale ranged from 0 to 100; the higher the score, the more intense the psychological distress. This questionnaire was translated into French and standardized with 16 000 Quebecois (Martin, Sabourin, & Gendreau, 1989; Tousignant & Kovess, 1985). The results revealed good reliability (*alphas* range from .72 to .89), and construct, convergent, and discriminant validities were all well established. The large Health Quebec Study (Tousignant & Kovess, 1985) has set 30 as the cutoff point for significant distress.

Marital Coping Questionnaire (MCQ) (Fleishman, 1984; Menaghan, 1982; Pearlin & Schooler, 1978) is an 18-item self-report questionnaire in which respondents indicate how frequently they engaged in each of a set of coping strategies when they were confronted with marital problems. Scoring was based on a Likert scale from 1 (not at all) to 5 (very often). The higher the score, the more a person used the strategy proposed. Exploratory and confirmatory factor analysis for this measure produced six reliable coping factors: seeking advice, emotional discharge, positive comparison, negotiation, resignation, and selective ignoring. Results revealed also good reliability (*alphas* range from .71 to .91; Fleishman, 1984). Convergent validity of the French version was also well established (Sabourin, Laporte, & Wright, 1990).

Procedure

Whether recruited from the community or the private clinic, couples followed the same procedures and measures. They answered the questionnaires in their homes and returned them separately by mail. A research assistant administered questionnaires to couples recruited from the community. To avoid having partners compare and discuss their results, they were told to answer the questionnaires alone. The couples also completed a consent form and a brief socio-demographic questionnaire. Any participant requesting a computerized report of the results was given one. Couples recruited from the private clinic were invited to participate when they were first interviewed by the admitting clinician (all psychologists with experience in marital therapy). The instruments were part of a battery gathered to enhance the information available from couple interviews.

RESULTS

Typology of Anger Profiles Within Couples

In order to explore and identify anger profiles within couples, we conducted couples' cluster analysis using, for each partner, the five indices derived from the IAEC: state anger, trait anger, anger-in, anger-out, and anger control. Clusters were obtained using Squared Euclidean Distance as a proximity measure and Ward's method[2] (SPSS, 1988). The selected four-group solution generated the following distribution of couples from the control group (recruited from the normal population), and from the clinical sample (seeking marital therapy): Type 1 (n = 69 couples, 55 control and 14 clinical), Type 2 (n = 51, 28 control and 23 clinical), Type 3 (n = 79, 26 control and 53 clinical), and Type 4 (n = 21, 1 control and 20 clinical). Means and standard deviations are reported in Table 1. Analysis of variance showed that there were no differences between the four groups on the sociodemographic variables.

A 4 (Group) × 2 (Sex) mixed design MANOVA, with Sex as the repeated measures factor, was conducted to assess group differences on the five anger variables and to establish the quality of the anger profiles. The minimal significance level of $p < .01$ was employed. A significant main effect ($p < .001$) for Group × Sex interaction, F (3,216) = 8.99, for Group, F (3,216) = 19.72, and for Sex, F (1,216) = 30.09 emerged from this initial analysis. These interactions, presented in Table 1, were significant on all variables except the state anger.

TABLE 1. Couple Clusters Emerging from Anger Profiles

	TYPE 1 (*n* = 69) M SD	TYPE 2 (*n* = 51) M SD	TYPE 3 (*n* = 79) M SD	TYPE 4 (*n* = 21) M SD	F (Gr. × Sex interaction)
State anger					
W	10.8 (2.7)	14.2 (6.5)	15.7 (7.2)	25.3 (9.7)	3.18
H	10.5 (1.2)	11.7 (3.0)	13.3 (4.7)	20.0 (7.8)	
Trait anger					
W	16.9 (4.1)	22.3 (5.1)	22.1 (4.9)	28.3 (6.3)	13.70***
H	15.6 (3.8)	15.1 (3.1)	21.5 (4.3)	22.1 (4.5)	
Anger-in					
W	14.5 (4.5)	17.0 (5.3)	17.1 (4.5)	16.8 (3.8)	5.33**
H	14.8 (3.9)	17.3 (4.2)	16.1 (4.1)	21.5 (3.8)	
Anger-out					
W	12.0 (3.3)	15.4 (3.9)	17.5 (4.1)	24.7 (6.0)	13.82***
H	13.3 (3.6)	11.9 (3.3)	18.2 (4.6)	19.5 (5.5)	
Anger control					
W	24.0 (3.9)	18.0 (3.6)	18.8 (5.0)	15.5 (3.8)	36.86***
H	24.0 (4.6)	26.8 (3.4)	18.4 (3.3)	23.8 (4.2)	

$^{**}p < .01$ $^{***}p < .001$

Furthermore, simple effects group for husbands and wives on state anger were significant, F (3,216) = 29.24 and F (3,216) = 32.89. To identify the source of the differences between clusters, Sheffé post-hoc tests ($p < .01$) were selected because the sample sizes were not equivalent. The four couple types differed significantly on almost every anger variable. The averages of these scales, seen in Table 1, revealed increasing distress in the quality of the anger profiles from Type 1 up to Type 4, with important sex differences on Types 2 and 4. The establishment of anger profiles through Spielberger's (1988) percentile scoring system generated interesting results (see Figure 1).

Type 1 spouses, which we will label "Relaxed Couples," were in the normal range on each anger scale (all between the 25th and 75th percentiles). Spouses reported feeling little anger towards each other. Their individual dispositions to experience anger, as measured by trait anger, appeared to be within the normal range. These couples also revealed an adequate pattern of anger expression. More specifically, both partners reported using anger-in, anger-out, and anger control expression within the acceptable limits.

FIGURE 1. Patterns of Couple's Anger Profiles. Percentiles Were Established According to Spielberger's Norms (1988)

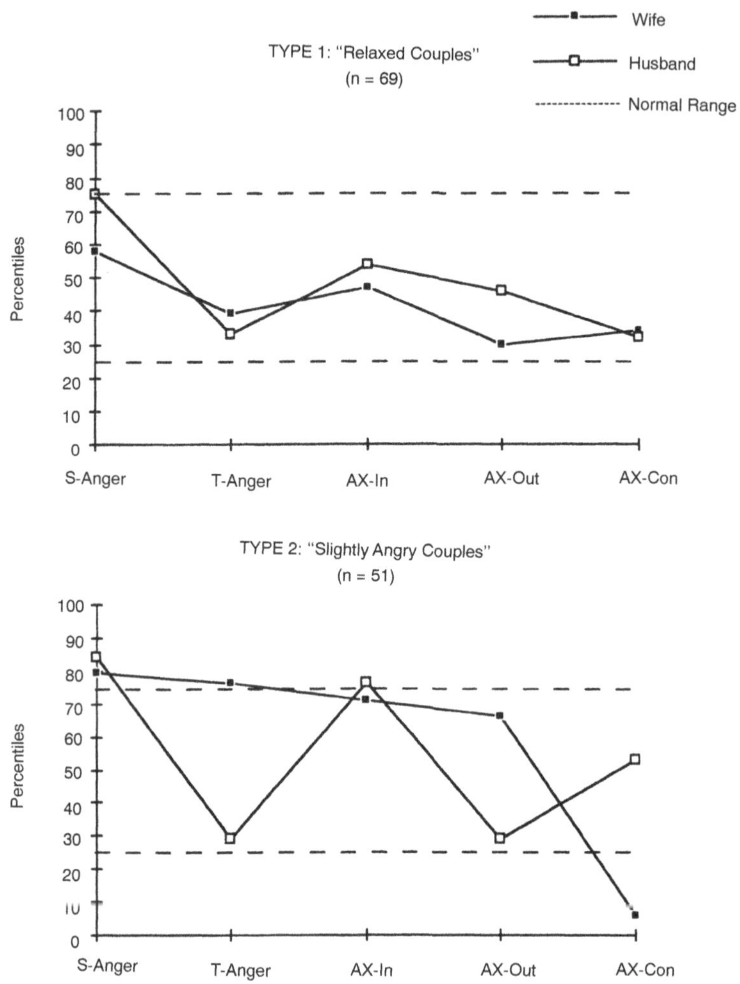

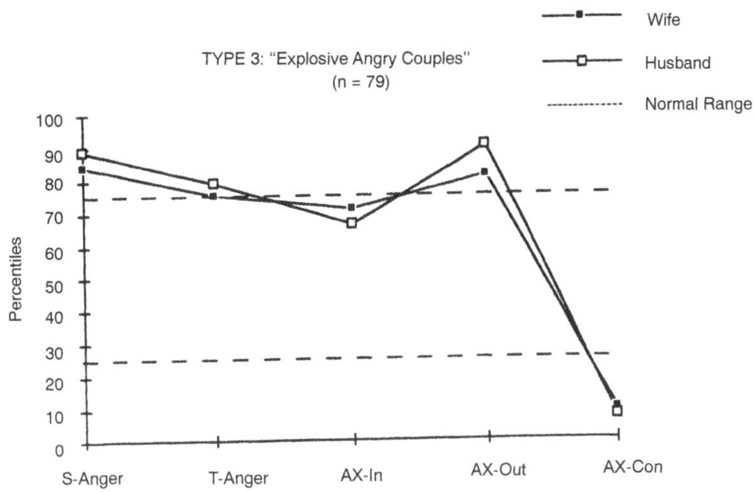

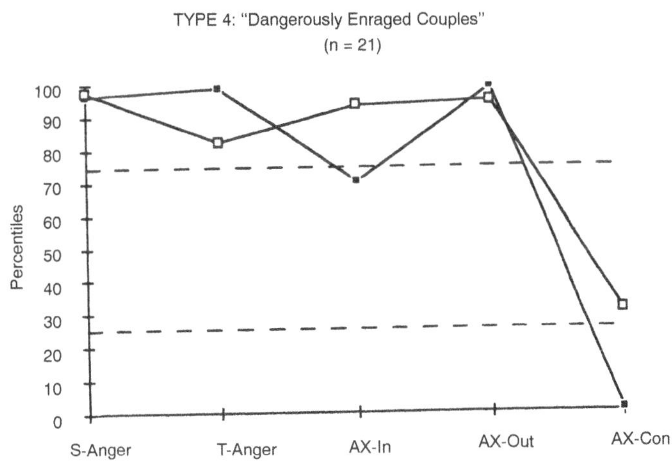

Type 2 partners, or "Slightly Angry Couples," were marked by the wives scoring ($p < .001$) slightly higher than their husbands on state, F (1,216) = 6.92, $p < .01$, trait, F (1,216) = 62.04, and anger-out expression, F (1,216) = 20.71. Wives in this group also reported less anger control expression than their husbands, F (1,216) = 113.73. The quality of Type 2 couples' anger dynamics is clearly illustrated by the percentile scores on the five IAEC scales presented in Figure 1. Wives reported feeling angry towards their partners and had high trait anger (both scales are above 75th). They reported high, though within normal limits, anger-in and anger-out expression (between 25th and 75th), but scored below the 25th percentile on the anger control scale, suggesting very poor control of anger expression strategies. Though husbands in group 2 reported trait anger within the normal range (between 25th and 75th), they felt angry towards their wives (above 75th) and tended greatly to hold in these feelings (above 75th) rather than outwardly express or control their anger (both between 25th and 75th). Compared with Type 1 raw scores, Type 2 wives reported higher trait anger, seemed to rely more on anger-out expression, and had poor control of anger expression, and Type 2 husbands more often suppressed and attempted to control anger.

Type 3 husbands and wives were labelled "Explosive Angry Couples," since both partners had similar stronger anger profiles. As observed in Figure 1, these spouses experienced intense angry feelings towards each other, demonstrated high trait anger, and often relied on anger-out expression (all three scales above 75th). They made efforts to hold in their anger (close to 70th) but rarely controlled it (close to 10th). Compared with Type 1 raw scores, both Type 3 spouses displayed significantly more angry feelings towards each other. They also had higher trait anger, scored higher on the anger-out scale and lower on the anger control scale than Type 1 spouses and Type 2 husbands.

Type 4 spouses, or "Dangerously Enraged Couples," revealed ill-adapted anger profiles, according to Spielberger's criteria. Figure 1 provides a clear portrait of the intensity of this group's anger dynamics. Spouses were very enraged towards each other, with scores above the 90th percentile on the state anger scale. The trait anger scores of 98th percentile for wives and 82nd for husbands suggested that both had personal dispositions to experience a great deal of frustration. Wives seemed prone to anger-out expression (98th) and, to a lesser extent, anger suppression strategies (70th), and almost never attempted to control their anger (1st). Husbands often resorted to anger-in (93rd) and anger-out expression (94th), and tried somewhat to control their anger (31st). Significant sex differences were also observed on the raw scores of all five anger variables ($p < .001$). Wives reported more state, $F(1,216) = 13.83$, trait, $F(1,216) = 18.75$, anger-out, $F(1,216) = 18.65$, and less anger-in, $F(1,216) = 14.01$, and anger control strategies, F (1,216) = 40.75, than their husbands did. Compared with the three other groups, Type 4 spouses reported much higher state and trait anger, and relied more often on anger-out expression with their partners, although differences between Type 3 and Type 4 husbands were not significant on state and anger-out. Type 4 husbands' anger-in scores were also higher than those of the other groups. Type 4 wives had poorer control of their anger than Type 1 women did; Type 4 husbands controlled their anger better than their Type 3 counterparts.

A Comparison of the Four Anger Profile Groups on Marital Adjustment, Psychiatric Symptoms, and Coping Skills

Analyses of variance were conducted to compare the four groups on dyadic adjustment, psychiatric symptoms and coping skills. Simple effects group with post-hoc comparisons and simple effects sex were also calculated. Means, standard deviations, and simple effects groups, for both husbands and wives, are reported in Table 2. These results were analyzed with the level of significance set at $p < .01$.

Dyadic Adjustment

ANOVA on marital adjustment indicated only a significant main effect for Group, F (3,216) = 41.49, $p < .001$. More specifically, Type 1 and Type 2 spouses were more satisfied according to their dyadic adjustment score than were Types 3 and 4. The first two groups (non-distressed) were above the clinical cut off point of 100, while last two groups (distressed) were below it. As noted in Table 2, however, dyadic adjustment averages decreased in gradients of about 10 points from Type 1 to Type 4 spouses. The level of marital adjustment per group can be summarized as follows: Type 1, "very satisfied"; Type 2, "moderately satisfied"; Type 3, "lightly unsatisfied"; Type 4, "very unsatisfied."

Psychological Distress

A 4 (Group) × 2 (Sex) mixed design MANOVA, with Sex as the repeated measures factor, was examined on the four scales of the Psychiatric Symptoms Index: depression, anxiety, hostility, and cogni-

TABLE 2. Mean, Standard Deviations and Group Differences on "External" Variables

	TYPE 1 (n = 69) M SD	TYPE 2 (n = 51) M SD	TYPE 3 (n = 79) M SD	TYPE 4 (n = 21) M SD	F (Simple effects Gr.)
Dyadic Adjustment					
W	115.9 (15.9)	104.6 (17.9)	91.4 (21.0)•	81.8 (14.1)•	30.99***
H	116.9 (13.5)	107.0 (17.0)	96.9 (17.3)•	84.0 (12.6)•	32.98***
Psychiatric Symptoms					
Depression					
W	22.9 (18.8)	31.6 (20.8)•	41.4 (24.3)•	61.1 (19.3)•	19.89***
H	17.6 (13.3)	23.9 (18.4)	27.5 (20.6)	41.4 (15.8)•	10.72***
Anxiety					
W	19.4 (15.8)	25.1 (17.7)	28.7 (20.1)	43.6 (21.1)•	9.69***
H	12.3 (9.9)	16.4 (14.4)	21.5 (15.6)	23.7 (14.2)	7.24***
Hostility					
W	23.0 (16.2)	31.7 (17.6)•	36.7 (18.7)•	59.5 (22.2)•	*4.95***
H	16.1 (10.3)	20.6 (14.2)	26.0 (16.0)	32.9 (13.5)•	
Cognitive disturbance					
W	22.6 (17.3)	27.9 (21.1)	30.9 (23.2)•	47.1 (29.3)•	7.08***
H	18.9 (16.3)	23.2 (18.0)	27.8 (20.7)	31.7 (21.6)•	3.88**
Coping skills					
Seeking advice					
W	7.1 (3.2)	7.8 (3.0)	9.2 (3.8)	9.7 (3.2)	8.68***
H	5.9 (2.6)	6.4 (2.8)	7.0 (2.7)	8.5 (2.7)	5.60**
Emotional discharge					
W	8.6 (2.9)	10.5 (2.9)	12.0 (3.1)	14.5 (3.3)	27.95***
H	7.6 (2.6)	9.0 (2.5)	10.4 (2.7)	10.7 (2.2)	18.47***
Positive comparison					
W	17.1 (3.7)	14.8 (4.6)	12.6 (4.5)	10.4 (3.9)	20.03***
H	17.0 (3.4)	14.9 (4.5)	13.1 (4.3)	10.8 (4.2)	16.19***
Negotiation					
W	16.2 (2.7)	15.2 (2.9)	14.5 (2.9)	14.1 (2.5)	5.78**
H	14.9 (3.6)	14.8 (3.4)	13.5 (3.0)	14.7 (2.6)	2.69
Resignation					
W	9.0 (2.6)	10.0 (2.8)	11.3 (3.0)	11.8 (3.4)	10.18***
H	9.4 (2.8)	11.3 (3.0)	11.2 (2.6)	14.4 (2.1)	18.06***
Selective ignoring					
W	9.3 (2.8)	8.8 (2.5)	9.3 (2.2)	9.5 (2.7)	.56
H	10.1 (2.7)	10.3 (3.0)	10.2 (2.2)	11.5 (2.4)	1.27

Note. Result in italics indicates a Group × Sex interaction.

• Indicates clinical scores (only available on first and second questionnaires)

$^{**}p < .01$ $^{***}p < .001$

tive disturbance. Results ($p < .001$) indicated a significant main effect for Group, F (3,215) = 6.69, and for Sex, F (1,215) = 21.33, as well as a significant Group × Sex interaction, F (3,215) = 2.38, $p < .01$. This interaction was however significant only on the hostility scale F (3,215) = 4.95, $p < .01$. Table 2 reveals significant simple effects group on all variables for each sex. A general increase in mean of psychological distress was associated with the couples' anger profiles from Type 1 to Type 4. Furthermore, simple effects sex revealed that all wives reported feeling more hostile and anxious than their partners did. In addition, Type 3 and Type 4 wives appeared to be more depressed than their husbands, all Fs (1,215) range from 7.84 to 35.36, $p < .01$.

Results generated the following clinical picture. Type 1 spouses were characterized by normal psychological adjustment, with means below 30. Although Type 2 spouses did not differ significantly from Type 1 spouses in post-hoc comparisons, increasing means were noted for both Type 2 sexes on psychiatric symptoms, while Type 2 wives scored above the clinical cutoff point of 30 on the depression and hostility scales. Type 3 partners reported feeling more depressed, anxious, and hostile than Type 1 spouses, but only Type 3 wives reported high (30+) depression, hostility, and cognitive disturbance symptomatology. Type 4 spouses demonstrated a level of psychological distress that clearly surpassed the clinical point on every scale except men's anxiety. The psychological distress of Type 4 wives was particularly striking. Type 4 spouses also scored higher than Types 1 and 2 on the depression, hostility, and anxiety scales, and Type 4 wives appeared to be more depressed and hostile than their Type 3 counterparts.

Marital Coping Efforts

A 4 (Group) × 2 (Sex) mixed design MANOVA, with Sex as the repeated measures factor, was completed on the six coping strategies: seeking advice, emotional discharge, positive comparison, negotiation, resignation, and selective ignoring. Results ($p < .001$) indicated a significant main effect for Group, F (3,208) = 6.32, and for Sex, F (1,208) = 16.27. Table 2 indicates significant simple effects group on all variables, except negotiation for husbands and selective ignoring for both spouses. The strongest sex differences were observed on the seeking advice and emotional discharge scales in that wives reported using these strategies more often than their husbands did, all *F*s (1,208) range from 9.40 to 39.05, $p < .01$.

Results indicate that Type 1 spouses attempted to use adequate marital coping skills. They usually coped with their marital problems through negotiation and positive comparison. Type 2 spouses also reported relying on relatively good coping skills, but post-hoc tests analysis indicated that they differed from Type 1 in that Type 2 wives tended more often to use emotional discharge strategies, while their husbands relied more often on resignation. Compared with Type 1 spouses, Types 3 and 4 reported more frequent use of seeking advice, resignation, and emotional discharge, and rarely used positive comparison. Furthermore, Type 4 spouses used positive comparison strategies less often than Type 2 spouses. Finally, contrasts between Types 3 and 4 revealed that Type 4 wives relied more on emotional discharge, while their husbands reported frequent reliance on resignation.

DISCUSSION

Despite the explosion of research on determinants of marital distress, there has been little systematic research on how couples experience and express their anger. This is surprising, given that the intensity and management of this emotion have often been linked to the escalation and de-escalation of abusive behavior (Burman et al., 1993). Moreover, excessive free-floating hostility has often been employed to explain both lack of progress in marital therapy and drops in constructive communication or affectionate and sexual exchanges (Gottman, 1994).

Our own clinical experience suggests that, in their marital interaction, couples do not just fall into a simple continuum of anger expression and emotional abuse, but that distinctive subgroups of couples' anger dynamics do exist. Along these lines, this study sought to identify different marital profiles of anger experience and expression. It also attempted to clarify how different anger profiles might be linked to couples' perceptions of the quality of their relationship, to their psychological distress, and to the coping skills they used in handling marital problems.

The first objective of this research was achieved as cluster analysis revealed four distinctive groups of couples based on their profiles of anger experience and expression. Also, as predicted, differences between the four groups in psychological and marital adjustment and in coping skills suggested different relationship dynamics. In sum, anger profiles showed increasing maladjustment from Type 1 to Type 4 spouses. Moreover, couple Types 1 and 2 appeared to have better marital relationships and fewer mental health problems, and coped more constructively with their conflicts than Types 3 and 4 did. These variables support the validity of the proposed clusters, which have been found to discriminate distressed from nondistressed couples in many studies (Bowman, 1990; Menaghan, 1984; Sabourin, Laporte, & Wright, 1990).

What types of couples were identified? The first group, "Relaxed Couples," showed a generally healthy profile. Type 1 partners did not feel constantly angry towards each other and did not demonstrate an individual disposition to experience great frustration. They appeared to communicate their anger in a balanced fashion and used an adequate mix of expression styles. These couples could express their anger with adequate control or choose to keep their feelings inside; their occasional quarrels were usually moderate. Their anger expression style co-varied with good coping efforts in which they often used negotiation or positive comparison of their relationships with other couples. Both partners were very satisfied with the quality of their relationships and did not report elevated psychological distress.

Little research to date has attempted to identify and study the positive side of anger. Type 1 spouses illustrated how a certain dose of anger is not always bad, and how anger does not always merit the label "negative emotion." Several studies have already underlined the importance of metacognitive processes in the development of conflicts during marital interaction (Alberts & Driscoll, 1992; Burman et al., 1993; Gottman, 1993; Sabourin et al., 1990). Future study with these couples could add measures of cognition related to their anger.

Type 2 or "Slightly Angry Couples" appeared to possess complementary anger dynamics. Only the wives reported high individual differences in proneness to anger as a personality trait. They felt angry towards their husbands and more often needed to suppress their anger and express sarcastic remarks (albeit within normal limits). Although Type 2 husbands experienced relatively high state anger, they did not report having high trait anger. Consequently, they seemed to prefer suppressing their anger. The manner in which both partners coped with their marital conflicts appeared to be as adaptive as Type 1, but wives more often resorted to free emotional discharge, while husbands tended to rely on resignation. This complementary style, in which a husband's profile appeared to counter-balance his wife's anger, did not appear to be problematic, since both partners reported moderate marital satisfaction. Because wives reported feeling mad and sad, however, it is tempting to conclude that they were more personally disturbed by their own dynamics.

Type 3 spouses, "Explosive Angry Couples," were characterized by intense and very similar anger profiles. They reported high personality trait anger and felt very angry towards their spouses. Both needed to express their anger with great intensity. Instead of trying to control themselves, they were prone to express their anger freely, mainly through sarcastic remarks or criticism. Both spouses seemed to be caught in an explosive dynamic, with strong psychological distress and pessimistic perceptions of their relationships. In coping with their conflicts, these couples tended to seek advice, discharge their problems freely, and be resigned.

All but one of the 21 Type 4 or "Dangerously Enraged Couples" were in marital therapy. Both Type 4 partners reported having very quick and bad tempers and were very sensitive to criticism, especially the wives. These couples appeared to be overcharged with conflicting intense feelings, and the manner in which they managed their fury or rage seemed very problematic. They excessively ventilated in a mean manner or held in their feelings towards their partners. Husbands tried a bit harder than their wives to keep their rage inside. These couples were not happy in their marriages and experienced high levels of psychiatric symptoms, particularly the wives. Like Type 3 couples, Type 4 spouses revealed a lot of difficulty in coping with their problems. Type 4 spouses were worse, however: the wives relying much more often on a free discharge of feelings, and their husbands relying more on resignation.

The two last groups, the "Explosive Angry Couples" and the "Dangerously Enraged Couples," were characterized by free-floating hostility mixed with mismanagement of marital conflicts, personal distress, and a lack of satisfaction with their close relationships. These observations confirmed other research, in which spouses in an emotionally chaotic relationship were much less satisfied than normal couples (Burman et al., 1993; Walker, 1995). It would be interesting to have observational marital interaction data to investigate whether problematic anger expression such as contempt and belligerence, identified by Jacobson et al. (1994), increased from "Explosive Angry Couples" to "Dangerously Enraged Couples." Further research could also explore whether anger, contempt, and belligerence are three distinct emotions, or are ordered on a continuum of varying intensity.

The present research provided some thought-provoking differences between husbands and wives in the way they express and experience anger. According to Spielberger's scoring system, Types 2 and 4 wives in our sample seemed to have a bit more maladaptive anger profile patterns than their husbands. We suggest extreme caution, however, before jumping to this conclusion. Literature on sex differences in affective dimensions such as anger revealed that results varied greatly from study to study (Fischer, Smith, Leonard, Fuqua, Campbell, & Masters, 1993). Certain inconsistencies could be explained by the nature of the sample and the context or situation in which people were studied. Furthermore, in complex couple dynamics, the outward expression of anger could be interpreted as an important healthy defense mechanism. In addition, this study did not gather observational data. It would be interesting to compare the views that couples had of their own interpersonal style with the objective perceptions of trained observers. Sometimes, particularly with spouses in crisis, the higher scores of wives might reflect accurate self-perceptions, while the lower scores of husbands might reflect underestimation of anger. On the other hand, cultural differences cannot be ruled out. Quebec women have profited enormously from the "quiet revolution," especially in the sphere of education. Social assertiveness and the expression of emotion by females is now more strongly encouraged and not necessarily seen as excessive. Without the more complete picture provided by observational data, reasons for consultation, and a couple's history of anger and violence, it is difficult to fully interpret the meaning of the present gender differences.

Our clinical sample did not include physically violent couples. These couples were automatically referred to therapists specializing in domestic violence. It would be intriguing to explore whether violent spouses fall into clusters 3 or 4, or exhibit another distinctive anger profile. Greene, Coles, and Johnson (1994) have reported that different anger expression patterns can be observed among interpersonally violent offenders. Personality assessment and physiological measures would probably be necessary, however, to discriminate other categories of physically aggressive spouses. Gottman et al. (1995) have found that the group of violent men exhibiting lowered heart rates were more verbally aggressive with their wives and others outside the family, demonstrated antisocial behavior and sadistic aggression, and were lower on dependency than the violent men exhibiting higher heart rates. The first type seemed to be in "cool control," much like a psychopath, while the second group were more emotionally chaotic and insecure. Following this research, these authors opened a debate about the appropriate therapy for the first group, since their problem appeared to be excessive control over their physiology, and not a lack of control. It would be interesting to study whether "cooler psychopathic husbands" could be associated with our clusters 3 or 4. We would expect these men to report fewer problems with anger management, but their wives would disagree.

In clinical practice, identification of the four types suggests that including the IAEC could help establish the intensity of a couple's crisis, its danger level, and its prognosis. The IAEC would also help in determining whether anger management should be a therapeutic objective and in evaluating the degree of progress in therapy. IAEC data would be analyzed in light of simultaneous assessment of the complementary dynamics of a couple's history, including the development of dangerous escalations of physical or verbal aggression and individual differences in proneness to anger as a personality trait.

In conclusion, the current research identified four different anger profiles in couples. These varied from low intensity, easily-managed anger in cluster 1 to high intensity, poorly-managed anger in cluster 4. We contend that the systematic assessment of couple and individual anger profiles will improve our understanding of couple dynamics. Complete models, however, must take into account sex differences, the constructive versus destructive impact of anger expression, and the balance of power within a couple to understand fully the function of anger in an intimate relationship.

NOTES

1. Some examples follow, with Spielberger's words in roman type and our additions italics: Instructions: When Angry or Furious *Towards My Partner*; Items: I withdraw from *him/her*. I make sarcastic remarks to *him/her*. I calm down faster than *my partner*.

2. Squared Euclidean Distance was used because it is a complete linkage procedure. Because of the information it provides on elevation, shape, and scatter (Everitt, 1979), we relied on it most heavily. Ward's method was used because it is recognized in maximizing the distance between clusters (SPSS, 1988). The agglomeration schedule revealed a relatively large increase in the value of the distance measure from the four-cluster to the three-cluster solution, suggesting that the four-cluster solution is more significant. In addition, the four-cluster solution provided a more even group size, whereas the three-cluster solution regrouped Types 1 and 2 into too large a group compared with Types 3 and 4. The four groups of couples have been compared on the clustering anger variables and on the additional "external variables." Differences found on the latter variables, however, support the validity of the clustering (Aldenderfer & Blashfield, 1984).

REFERENCES

Alberts, J. K., & Driscoll, G. (1992). Containment versus escalation: The trajectory of couples' conversational complaints. *Western Journal of Communication, 56,* 394-412.

Aldenderfer, M. S., & Blashfield, R. K. (1984). *Cluster analysis.* Newbury Park, CA: Sage.

Baillargeon, J., Dubois, G., & Marineau, R. (1986). Traduction française de l'échelle d'ajustement dyadique. *Sciences et Comportement, 18,* 25-34.

Bélanger, C., Sabourin, S., & Wright, J. (1993). Les développements récents dans l'étude de la communication et de la détresse maritale: Évolution ou révolution? *Psychologie Canadienne, 34,* 3-25.

Boland, J. P., & Follingstad, D. R. (1987). The relationship between communication and marital satisfaction: A review. *Journal of Sex and Marital Therapy, 13,* 286-313.

Bowman, M. L. (1990). Coping efforts and marital satisfaction: Measuring marital coping and its correlates. *Journal of Marriage and Family, 52,* 463-470.

Bradbury, T. N., & Fincham, F. D. (1990). Attributions in marriage: Review and critique. *Psychological Bulletin, 107,* 3-33.

Burman, B., John, R. S., & Margolin, G. (1992). Observed patterns of conflict in violent, nonviolent, and nondistressed couples. *Behavioral Assessment, 14,* 15-37.

Burman, B., Margolin, G., & John, R. S. (1993). America's angriest home videos: Behavioral contingencies observed in home reenactments of marital conflict. *Journal of Consulting and Clinical Psychology, 61,* 28-39.

Derogatis, L., Lipman, R., & Rickels, D. (1974). The hopkins symptom checklist: A self-report symptom inventory. *Behavioral Sciences, 19,* 1-15.

Everitt, B. S. (1979). Unresolved problems in cluster analysis. *Biometrics, 35,* 169-181.

Fischer, P., Smith, R. J., Leonard, E., Fuqua, D. L., Campbell, J. L., & Masters, M.A. (1993). Sex differences on affective dimensions: Continuing examination. *Journal of Counseling & Development, 71,* 440-443.

Fleishman, J. A. (1984). Personality characteristics and coping patterns. *Journal of Health and Social Behavior, 25,* 229-244.

Floyd, F. J., & Markman, H. J. (1983). Observational biases in spouse observation: Toward a cognitive/behavioral model of marriage. *Journal of Consulting and Clinical Psychology, 51,* 450-457.

Fuqua, D. R., Leonard, E., Masters, M. A., Smith, R. J., Cambell, J. L., & Fischer, P. C. (1991). A structural analysis of the State-trait anger expression inventory. *Educational and Psychological Measurement, 51,* 439-446.

Gottman, J. M. (1993). A theory of marital dissolution and stability. *Journal of Family Psychology, 7,* 57-75.

Gottman, J. M. (1994). *What predicts divorce?* Hillsdale, NJ: LEA Publishers.

Gottman, J. M., Jacobson, N. S., Rushe, R., Shortt, J., Babcock, J., La Taillande, J. J., & Walz, J. (1995). The relationship between heart rate reactivity, emotionally aggressive behavior, and general violence in batterers. *Journal of Family Psychology, 9,* 227-248.

Gottman, J. M., & Krokoff, L. J. (1989). Marital interaction and satisfaction: A longitudinal view. *Journal of Consulting and Clinical Psychology, 57,* 47-52.

Greene, A. F., Coles, C., & Johnson, E. H. (1994). Psychopathology and anger in interpersonal violence offenders. *Journal of Clinical Psychology, 50,* 906-912.

Ilfeld, F. W. (1976). Further validation of a psychiatric index in a normal population. *Psychological Reports, 39,* 1215-1228.

Jacobson, N. S., Gottman, J. M., Waltz, J., Rushe, R., Babcock, J., & Holtzworth-Munroe, A. (1994). Affect, verbal content and psychophysiology in the arguments of couples with a violent husband. *Journal of Consulting and Clinical Psychology, 62,* 982-988.

Karney, B. R., & Bradbury, T. N. (1995). The longitudinal course of marital quality and stability: A review of theory, method, and research. *Psychological Bulletin, 118,* 3-34.

Krokoff, L. J. (1991). Communication orientation as a moderator between strong negative affect and marital satisfaction. *Behavioral Assessment, 13,* 51-65.

Laughrea, K., Bélanger, C., Sabourin, S., Lussier, Y., & Wright, J. (1992). L'effet des attributions sur l'évolution de la détresse conjugale. *Revue Québécoise de Psychologie, 13,* 90-104.

Laughrea, K., Bélanger, C., & Wright, J. (1996). L'inventaire de l'expérience de la colère en situation sociale et conjugale: Validation auprès de la population adulte québécoise. *Sciences et Comportement, 25,* (1), 71-94.

Laughrea, K., Bélanger, C., Wright, J., & McDuff, P. (1997). L'étude de la colère au sein des relations conjugales. *International Journal of Psychology, 32,* 155-167.

Lloyd, S. A. (1990). Conflict types and strategies in violent marriages. *Journal of Family Violence, 5,* 269-284.

Margolin, G., John, R. S., & Gleberman, L. (1988). Affective responses to conflictual discussions in violent and nonviolent couples. *Journal of Consulting and Clinical Psychology, 56,* 24-33.

Margolin, G., John, R. S., & O'Brien, M. (1989). Sequential affective patterns as a function of marital conflict style. *Journal of Social and Clinical Psychology, 8,* 45-61.

Markman, H. J. (1991). Constructive marital conflict is not an oxymoron. *Behavioral Assessment, 13,* 83-96.

Martin, F., Sabourin, S., & Gendreau, P. (1989). Les dimensions de la détresse psychologique: Une analyse factorielle confirmatoire de type hiérarchique. *International Journal of Psychology, 24,* 571-584.

Menaghan, E. (1982). Measuring coping effectiveness: A panel analysis of marital problems and coping efforts. *Journal of Health and Social Behavior, 23,* 220-234.

Murphy, C., & O'Leary, K. D. (1989). Psychological aggression predicts physical aggression in early marriage. *Journal of Clinical and Consulting Psychology, 57,* 579-582.

O'Leary, K. D., Malone, J., & Tyree, A. (1994). Physical aggression in early marriage: Prerelationship and relationship effects. *Journal of Consulting and Clinical Psychology, 62,* 594-602.

O'Leary, K. D., & Vivian, D. (1990). Physical aggression in marriage. In F. D. Fincham & T. N. Bradbury (Eds.), *The psychology of marriage: Basic issues and applications* (pp. 323-348). NY: The Guilford Press.

Pearlin, L. I., & Schooler, C. (1978). The structure of coping. *Journal of Health and Social Behavior, 19,* 2-21.

Sabourin, S., Laporte, L., & Wright, J. (1990). Problem solving self-appraisal and coping efforts in distressed and nondistressed couples. *Journal of Marital and Family Therapy, 16,* 89-97.

Sabourin, S., Lussier, Y., Laplante, B., & Wright, J. (1990). Unidimensional and multidimensional models of dyadic adjustment: A hierarchical reconciliation. *Psychological Assessment: Journal of Consulting and Clinical Psychology, 3,* 333-337.

Spanier, G. B. (1976). Measuring dyadic adjustment: New scales for assessing the quality of marriage and similar dyads. *Journal of Marriage and the Family, 38,* 15-28.

Spanier, G. B., & Thompson, L. (1982). A confirmatory analysis of the dyadic adjustment scale. *Journal of Marriage and the Family, 44,* 731-738.

Spielberger, C. D. (1988). *State-trait anger expression inventory* (STAXI). Odessa, FL: Psychological Assessment Resources.

Tousignant, M., & Kovess, V. (1985). L'épidémiologie en santé mentale: Le cadre conceptuel de l'enquête Santé Québec. *Sociologie et Sociétés, 17,* 15-26.

Walker, L. E. A. (1995). Current perspectives on men who batter women–implications for intervention and treatment to stop violence against women: Comment on Gottman et al. (1995). *Journal of Family Psychology, 9,* 264-271.

Who's Afraid of Intimacy?

Jeffrey S. Applegate

SUMMARY. This article employs concepts from object relations theory, attachment theory, and a psychodynamic-behavioral-systemic model of couple conflict and intimacy in constructing an integrative conceptual framework for clinical assessment and intervention with severely conflicted couples. The explication of theory is punctuated by excerpts from Edward Albee's play, "Who's Afraid of Virginia Woolf?" that exemplify key dynamics. This synthesis of theory and its dramatized expression is followed by some recommendations for clinical practice. *[Article copies available for a fee from The Haworth Document Delivery Service: 1-800-342-9678. E-mail address: <getinfo@haworthpressinc.com> Website: <http://www.HaworthPress.com>]*

KEYWORDS. Intimacy, attachment, couple conflict, couples therapy

With his characteristic flair for conceptualizing through paradox, the British psychoanalyst D. W. Winnicott (1958) noted that the capacity to be alone derives from repeated early experiences of a sense of

---

Jeffrey S. Applegate, DSW, is Professor, Graduate School of Social Work and Social Research, Bryn Mawr College, 300 Airdale Road, Bryn Mawr, PA 19010. He is a Distinguished Practitioner in the Social Work Division of the National Academies of Practice.

[Haworth co-indexing entry note]: "Who's Afraid of Intimacy?" Applegate, Jeffrey S. Co-published simultaneously in *Journal of Couples Therapy* (The Haworth Press, Inc.) Vol. 9, No. 1/2, 2000, pp. 109-126; and: *Couples Connecting: Prerequisites of Intimacy* (ed: Barbara Jo Brothers) The Haworth Press, Inc., 2000, pp. 109-126. Single or multiple copies of this article are available for a fee from The Haworth Document Delivery Service [1-800-342-9678, 9:00 a.m. - 5:00 p.m. (EST). E-mail address: getinfo@haworthpressinc.com].

separateness while in the intimate presence of another, usually the primary caregiver. This formulation suggests that only when able to experience personal autonomy in the benign presence of another can the developing child feel safe enough to engage in true intimacy. In the ideal developmental scenario, the child learns to experience autonomy without fearing abandonment and connectedness without fearing the loss of self through merger.

Of course, ideal development is a fiction. In real life no one ever completely reconciles the life-long dialectic between autonomy and intimacy, and, as adults, people typically bring residual anxiety about intimacy and its vicissitudes to their closest dyadic partnerships, including marriage (Shor & Sanville, 1978). If early development in both partners has been "good enough," they can tolerate and manage intimacy anxiety and its associated defenses in the context of a relatively non-conflicted committed relationship. But when early development has been compromised by interpersonal deprivation or trauma, anxiety about self-annihilation through abandonment or merger can send the autonomy-intimacy dialectic spinning out of control into a confusing and conflict-ridden spiral of reciprocal projective identifications. Trapped in a relational catch-22, couples often come for help when the level of conflict in their relationship has become unbearable. Such couples present formidable challenges to clinicians attempting to assist them.

This article employs Winnicott's ideas, selected concepts from attachment theory, and Feldman's (1979) psychodynamic-behavioral-systemic model of couple conflict and intimacy in proposing an integrative framework for clinical assessment and intervention with troubled couples. An explication of theory will be punctuated by excerpts from "Who's Afraid of Virginia Woolf?" Edward Albee's (1962/1983) award-winning play about a tortuous, fateful night in the life of a couple mired in repetitive cycles of destructive conflict. The intent of this synthesis of theory and its dramatized expression is to facilitate reflective consideration by clinicians of ways in which they can transpose the proposed conceptual framework to their own practice.

THE DEVELOPMENTAL DIALECTIC

The Greek philosopher Empedocles, born in 495 B.C., believed that two fundamental principles govern the life of the universe. One principle, *philia* (love), strives to unite disparate elements into larger unities. The other, *neikos* (strife), seeks to dissolve such unities in order to separate their elements. Empedocles conceived of these principles as finding expression in ceaselessly alternating periods when one or the other is in ascendancy. In "Analysis Terminable and Interminable," Freud (1937/1963) drew parallels between these principles and the two "primal instincts," Eros and destructiveness (libido and aggression, respectively), that he believed to govern psychological life. Echoing Empedocles, he suggested that Eros "strives to combine existing phenomena into ever greater unities," whereas destructiveness "seeks to dissolve these combinations and destroy the structures to which they have given rise" (p. 264).

Extending the application of Freud's dual drive theory to ego psychology, Blanck and Blanck (1979) suggest that libido is but one aspect of the larger human urge to fuse with another while aggression derives from an equally powerful urge to separate. Angyal's (1973) concepts of autonomy and homonomy, describing in turn motivations to differentiate and those to join or connect with others, also capture these transacting dimensions of human life and behavior.

Contemporary object relations theorists have attempted to map the intrapsychic correlates of these two overarching processes. Such concepts as psychological symbiosis and separation-individuation (Mahler, Pine, & Bergman, 1975) now stand as established elements in the lexicon of psychoanalytic developmental psychology. The achievement of a capacity to differentiate internalized mental representations of oneself from representations of others is viewed as a benchmark of psychological health, as is the capacity to tolerate periodically the blurring or temporary merger of self and object images. In addition to offering a conception of how psychological development unfolds, an understanding of such phenomena helps clinicians attend to the dynamics of closeness and distance as they express themselves in clients' lives and relationships, including the clinical relationship.

Despite an implicit recognition that adaptive human functioning expresses elements of both autonomy and merger, there is a tendency to view these phenomena in a dichotomous, polarized fashion. This tendency surfaces in current psychodynamic conceptions of development. Mahler and her associates (1975), for example, hypothesize that normal development moves infants from early states of undifferentiation toward separation and individuation of self from object images. Stern (1985), in contrast, suggests that infants are born with a differentiated sense of self and object images and move toward a capacity for merger experiences only after later cognitive and emotional development enables them to do so. Subscription to one or the other of these views can lead to different conceptions of psychological health and to different ways of understanding and intervening with clients.

Elsewhere I have called for a conceptual synthesis of these two perspectives that acknowledges the life-long interplay between union and separation that occurs at both the interpersonal and intrapsychic levels (Applegate, 1993). Drawing on Ogden's (1990a, 1990b) work, I suggest that thinking of the relationship between autonomy and intimacy as expressions of a developmental dialectic can be useful theoretically and clinically. A dialectic is a process in which two apparently opposing concepts each creates, preserves, and negates the other in ongoing dynamic interaction. In dialectics, meaning accrues from difference. As applied to autonomy and intimacy, a sense of separateness is possible only in relation to a sense of connectedness to another. These two states are at once distinct and inseparable.

With this dialectical conception, we must leave the conceptual high ground of linear thinking and enter the swampy labyrinths of paradox. And so it is that Winnicott (1958) comes to his curious statement that the capacity to be alone can be developed only in the presence of someone. With this idea he attempts to articulate "the separation that is not a separation but a form of union" (Winnicott, 1971a, p. 98), a state in which one experiences oneself as simultaneously distinct from and merged with another. Grotstein (1989) elaborates, describing this dialectic as "the ambiguous, twofold phenomenological aspects of early development in which an inchoate, canny, and separated self is simultaneously and ambiguously connected in the state of fusion with its mother and vacillates back and forth between these two states and/or may experience them simultaneously" (p. 136).

Winnicott (1971a) believed this dialectic to occur in a hypothetical intermediate area between representations of self and other which he termed "potential space." This space "both joins and separates the infant . . . and the mother" (Winnicott, 1971b, p. 107) in the infant's object world. This is the realm of the transitional object, the stuffed toy or blanket that simultaneously symbolizes the infant (in that he or she imbues it with meaning and self-soothing qualities) and the other (in that it is also an object in the external world). Thus, this object comes to stand for "separateness in unity, unity in separateness" (Ogden, 1990b, p. 212).

Applying these ideas to couple relationships, Shor and Sanville (1978) posit a dialectical spiral of intimacy and autonomy and employ a metaphor from genetics to describe how it works. Both within and between partners in a healthy couple, they suggest, a double helix comprised of oscillating mental states of closeness and distance spirals in constant dynamic synchrony. Never perfect, this synchrony can go awry in various phases of any couple's relationship, producing temporary imbalances in the tolerance in each for closeness and distance. In those couples where one or both partners bring early developmental vulnerabilities, the "helix" can be pulled into chaotic dys-synchrony, resulting in persistently repetitive, often escalating cycles of destructive conflict. Such vulnerabilities often stem from early disturbances in attachment.

ATTACHMENT THEORY AND COUPLE RELATIONSHIPS

One variant of object relations theory that is particularly helpful in explicating the dynamics of troubled couples is the theory of attachment proposed by Bowlby (1977, 1988). While theorists like Winnicott, Mahler, and Stern concentrate on explicating the intrapsychic dynamics among mental representations of self and other, Bowlby focuses on the behavioral manifestations of closeness and distance between people. Drawing on developmental biology, ethology, cognitive concepts, and control theory, Bowlby (1977) conceives of attachment theory as a way of understanding "the propensity of human beings to make strong affectional bonds to particular others and of explaining the many forms of emotional distress and personality disturbance, including anxiety, anger, depression and emotional detachment, to which unwilling separation and loss give rise" (p. 201).

Attachment behavior results in a person achieving and sustaining proximity to some other preferred individual who is usually seen as stronger or wiser. First manifested between infants and their primary caregivers, early patterns of attachment tend to persist throughout the life span, and, in adults, are likely to shape dynamics of later intimate partnerships. When early experiences with caregivers have provided a firmly attached "secure base" from which to begin to explore the world, the infant can be said to experience secure attachment. In the absence of a secure base, one of several expressions of separation anxiety, and associated defensive postures, results. In anxious attachment, the child appears to be chronically fearful of losing the attachment figure, and his or her threshold for tolerating separation is low. In compulsive self-reliance, the fear of loss expresses itself in a defensive avoidance of rejection by withdrawing from the close other. In compulsive caregiving, the child seeks little from others but, through reaction formation, becomes overly concerned about their well being. Finally, the emotionally detached child, probably the subject of chronic early deprivation and rejection, appears incapable of developing a stable affectional bond with another and keeps his or her distance (Bacal, 1990).

In adults, early difficulties with secure attachment tend to coalesce into primary relational styles of either anxious ambivalence or emotional avoidance (Sperling & Berman, 1994). Anxious/ambivalent adults tend to be needy, clinging, emotionally volatile, and demanding of attention. Avoidant individuals, in contrast, tend to be emotionally self-sufficient, detached, cerebral, and apparently dismissive of attention from others. Such individuals often "find" each other and form partnerships that permit them, through projective identification, to express the unconscious "flip side" of their defensive postures. The anxious/ambivalent partner, for example, projects fears of closeness and affective impoverishment onto the detached partner, whose behavior in turn expresses these unconscious dynamics. Similarly, the detached partner finds in the needy, highly emotional partner a mirror for the longings that he or she can neither "own" consciously nor express safely. Both experience separation anxiety, but each defensively wards if off through the complex choreography of this systemic dance.

INTIMACY AND ITS VICISSITUDES

In the conceptual framework of autonomy and intimacy as aspects of an oscillating developmental dialectic, Bowlby's work addresses issues of attachment and anxiety aroused by its absence. An understanding of the dynamics of couples in conflict also requires attention to human longings for autonomy and anxiety associated with threats to states of separateness. In focusing on intimacy anxiety, Feldman

(1979) offers an integrative conceptual model for considering this "pole" of the dialectic. He suggests that couples unconsciously identify an acceptable or tolerable level of intimacy in their relationship and establish a set of relational rules that, over time, become calibrated to preserve this safe level. Mature couples strike a balance that fulfills wishes for intimacy while warding off associated fears of loss of self through merger.

For couples in which the sense of a separate self in one or both partners is fragile, threats to autonomy result in intimacy anxiety that can set of repetitive cycles of nonproductive conflict. To describe these cycles, Feldman employs concepts from social learning theory. As partners' sense of separateness is threatened, intimacy anxiety escalates. In order to reduce this anxiety, one partner initiates conflict designed to create distance. As distance increases, intimacy anxiety diminishes, the partners become more comfortable, and the wish for intimacy re-emerges. This re-emergence stimulates moves toward conciliation in one of the partners. If the non-initiating partner remains more fearful and anxious than the initiator, another cycle begins. These patterns typically become entrenched, repetitive, and increasingly conflictual and rigidify into persistent patterns of reinforcement and negative feedback. Borrowing a metaphor from systems theory, Feldman (1979) refers to such patterns as artifacts of an "intrapsychic-interpersonal feedback loop." As he puts it, "intrapsychic anxiety stimulates interpersonal defensive behavior, and this in turn reinforces the persistence of the anxiety" (p. 77). If the intimacy anxiety fails to be contained systemically within agreed-upon limits, increasingly destructive feedback spirals, or "runaways," can result.

WHO'S AFRAID OF INTIMACY?

The types of couples and relational patterns described here will be familiar to clinicians. Often characterized as pursuer-distancer or hysterical-obsessive pairs, these couples appear to have forged unconscious covenants designed to maintain a cybernetic homeostasis in their relationships. But, in their extreme manifestations, such relationships become unstable over time and are highly vulnerable to a variety of life transitions, stresses, or crises.

Perhaps nowhere else in popular culture do we encounter a more pointed example of such a couple relationship than in Edward Albee's

(1962/1983) moving drama, "Who's Afraid of Virginia Woolf?" Adapted for film in 1968, this story of a disastrous night in the life of a severely conflicted couple provided the vehicle for an Oscar-winning performance by Elizabeth Taylor. Taylor plays Martha, 52 year-old daughter of the president of a small New England college and wife of George, an associate professor of history there. George, played by Richard Burton, is a brooding, preoccupied, cerebral 46 year-old man who appears stifled and beaten down by his life, his stalled career, and his marriage. Martha, in contrast, is loud, boozy, overbearing, and provocative, apparently raging against the emptiness of her life and her marriage. Both routinely drink too much and, in so doing, ignite cycles of verbally assaultive anger punctuated by brief and anxiety-provoking periods of rapprochement.

On the night depicted in the play, we find George and Martha returning from a college party for new faculty given by Martha's father. Without George's knowledge, Martha has invited a new assistant professor, Nick, and his wife Honey, both in their twenties, to come for a nightcap. Nick, played in the movie by George Segal, is an ambitious, athletic, and virile young man who has caught Martha's eye at the party. Honey, acted by Sandy Dennis, is his docile, ingratiating, overly-polite and mousy wife, given to bouts of nausea and swooning. Over the course of the play it becomes increasingly clear that Nick represents the aggressive phallic potency that George denies in himself, whereas Honey mirrors the passive dependency that Martha defends against through her brash presentation. By accepting the post-party invitation, this young couple steps into the maelstrom of one of George and Martha's most decisive, alcohol-fueled battles. A series of games ensues, symbolic of the system games George and Martha have constructed to both preserve and negate their fragile intimacy. On this night, the rules of a pivotal game are broken.

Apparently unable to have children, George and Martha have conceived an imaginary son, a perfect, golden boy who serves both as a transitional object attachment (Winnicott, 1953) and as a triangulated "other" designed to stabilize their precarious dyadic balance. This imaginary son, now an adolescent, has been their secret, part of the closed system of their relationship. Inebriated and tired, they begin fighting before Nick and Honey arrive. As their anger escalates, George warns Martha not to tell the prospective guests about their "son," thus unconsciously inviting her to do so:

*GEORGE: Just don't start in on the bit about the kid, that's all.
MARTHA: What do you take me for?
GEORGE: Much too much.
MARTHA (*really angered*): Yeah? Well, I'll start in on the kid if I want to (p. 18).

Throughout the play we witness cycles like those Feldman (1979) describes. We see Martha–the anxious/ambivalent partner in attachment terms–reach for symbiotic closeness while we watch George, the avoidant partner, retreat to preserve a tolerable level of intimacy. As the play opens, Martha demands that George read her mind (merge with her) by knowing the name of a movie she can't recall.

Walking in the front door of their house after the party, she begins:

*MARTHA (*Looks about the room. Imitates Bette Davis*): What a dump. Hey, what's that from? 'What a dump!'
GEORGE: How would I know what . . . .
MARTHA: Ah, come on! What's it from? *You* know. . . .
GEORGE: . . . Martha. . . .

When he fails to meet her demand, she lashes out in anxious rage:

*MARTHA: WHAT'S IT FROM, FOR CHRIST'S SAKE?
GEORGE (*Wearily*): What's what from?
MARTHA: I just told you; I just did it. 'What a dump!' Hunh? What's that from?
GEORGE: I haven't the faintest idea what. . . .
MARTHA: Dumbbell! It's from some goddamn Bette Davis picture . . . some goddamn Warner Brothers epic. . . . (pp. 3 & 4).

Sounding like many distressed couples seen in clinical settings, Martha and George proceed to "split" their perceptions of each other down a polarized fault line as projective identification becomes operative. This is the juncture at which clinicians begin to hear couples declare: "You *always* do this" and "you *never* do that."

*MARTHA: Well, what's the name of the picture?
GEORGE: I really don't know, Martha. . . .

MARTHA: Well, think!
GEORGE: I'm tired, dear . . . it's late . . . and besides. . . .
MARTHA: I don't know what you're so tired about . . . you haven't *done* anything all day; you didn't have any classes, or anything.
GEORGE: Well, I'm tired. . . . If your father didn't set up these goddamn Saturday night orgies all the time. . . .
MARTHA: That's too bad about you, George. . . .
GEORGE (*Grumbling*): Well, that's how it is, anyway.
MARTHA: You didn't *do* anything; you never *do* anything; you never *mix.* You just sit around and *talk.*
GEORGE: What do you want me to do? Do you want me to act like you? Do you want me to go around all night *braying* at everybody, the way you do?
MARTHA (*Braying*): I DON'T BRAY! (pp. 6 & 7).

Later, in a scene that takes place in their upstairs bedroom while they get ready to receive their guests, they seek to reduce the separation anxiety aroused by their conflict in a brief moment of intimacy, initiated by Martha. First, the conflict escalates:

*MARTHA: Uh . . . you make me puke!
GEORGE (Thinks about it . . . then . . .): That wasn't a very nice thing to say, Martha.
MARTHA: That wasn't *what?*
GEORGE: . . . a very nice thing to say.
MARTHA: I like your anger. I think that's what I like about you most . . . your anger. You're such a . . . simp! You don't even have the . . . the . . . the what?
GEORGE: . . . guts? . . . . (pp. 13-14).

George's humorous answer defuses the anger and is followed by a brief period of playful rapprochement that triggers intimacy anxiety and prompts George to retreat.

---

*MARTHA: PHRASEMAKER! (*Pause . . . then they both laugh*)
Hey, put some more ice in my drink, will you? You never put any ice in my drink. Why is that, hunh?
GEORGE: I always put ice in your drink. You eat it, that's all. It's that habit you have . . . chewing your ice cubes . . . like a cocker spaniel. You'll crack your big teeth.
MARTHA: THEY'RE MY BIG TEETH!
GEORGE: Some of them . . . some of them (p. 14).

And a few moments later–

*MARTHA: Well . . . you're going bald.
GEORGE: So are you. (*Pause . . . they both laugh*) Hello, honey.
MARTHA: Hello. C'mon over here and give your Mommy a big sloppy kiss.
GEORGE: . . . oh, now. . . .
MARTHA: I WANT A BIG SLOPPY KISS!
GEORGE: (*Preoccupied*) I don't *want* to kiss you, Martha. Where *are* these people? Where are these *people* you invited over?

[They return to the living room]

*MARTHA: They stayed on to talk to Daddy. . . . They'll be here. . . . Why don't you want to kiss me?
GEORGE (*Too matter-of-fact*): Well, dear, if I kissed you I'd get all excited . . . I'd get beside myself, and I'd take you, by force, right here on the living room rug, and then our little guests would walk in, and . . . well, just think what your father would say about *that*.
Martha: You pig!
George (*Haughtily*) Oink! Oink! (pp. 15-16).

From this breach in the intimacy initiated by Martha's invitation they return to bitter, angry dialogue and a regressive spiral escalates.

This exchange epitomizes feelings and behavior similar to those belonging to what Melanie Klein (1975) termed the paranoid-schizoid position, or what Winnicott (1963) referred to in less pathologizing language as the stage of pre-concern. In this relational mode the other is seen to exist not as an experiencing subject but as an invulnerable object, worthy of neither guilt nor reparation, or is treated as though he or she did not exist at all. A series of Martha's caustically dismissive remarks to Geroge clearly illustrate this dynamic.

> *MARTHA: I swear . . . if you existed I'd divorce you. . . . I can't even see you . . . I haven't been able to see you for years. . . . I mean, you're a blank, a cipher . . . a zero. . . . (pp. 16-17).

The guests, Honey and Nick, arrive at the crescendo of another angry interchange, and a brief period of feigned pleasant greetings and strained politeness soon deteriorates into vitriolic exchanges between Martha and George. These focus primarily on glorifying Martha's father and demeaning George for his lack of ambition and accomplishment. After a few minutes Martha and Honey excuse themselves to go upstairs and freshen up. George again warns Martha not to reveal their secret, again baiting her to do so. While Martha and Honey are absent, George and Nick engage in repartee whose thrust is that Nick is ambitious to get ahead at the college while George, threatened by this new interloper, tries to assert his dominance through hostile intimidation and word games. The conversation gets around to children; we learn that Nick and Honey have none. Nick asks George whether he and Martha have children, and George teases back, "That's for me to know and you to find out" (Albee, 1962/1983, p. 39).

When Martha and Honey reappear, Martha has changed into a strikingly seductive outfit and engages Nick in some flirtatiously suggestive conversation. Soon she begins to compare George unfavorably to Nick, making increasingly disparaging remarks about George's sexual prowess. George begins to seethe, disappears for a few minutes, then returns quietly while the other three are laughing and making jokes at his expense. Walking into the room, he raises a shotgun

---

and aims it at the back of Martha's head. All three turn simultaneously to notice this and scream in horror. George "fires" the gun, and out of the barrel explodes a large umbrella. Once Martha begins to compose herself, gasping, she begins to laugh. This triggers another brief move toward intimacy between them, initiated by Martha and abruptly foreclosed by George.

> *MARTHA (*Giggling*): You bastard.
> HONEY (*Wanting attention*): I've *never* been so frightened . . . never.
> NICK: This is quite a gadget.
> GEORGE (*Leaning over* Martha): You liked that, did you?
> MARTHA: Yeah . . . that was pretty good. (*Softer*) C'mon . . . give me a kiss.
> GEORGE (*Indicating* Nick *and* Honey): Later, sweetie. (*But* Martha *will not be dissuaded. They kiss,* George *standing, leaning over* Martha's *chair. She takes his hand, places it on her stage-side breast. He breaks away*) Oh-ho! That's what you're after, is it? What are we going to have . . . blue games for the guests? Hunh? Hunh?
> MARTHA (*angry-hurt*): You . . . prick!
> GEORGE (*A Pyrrhic victory*): Everything in its place, Martha . . . everything in its own good time.
> MARTHA (*An unspoken epithet*): You. . . . (pp. 58-59).

Predictably, Martha has told Honey the secret, confiding that she and George have a "son" who is to return the next day to celebrate his birthday. She thus breaks a fundamental rule in one of the couple's most sustaining marital games. They have colluded in opening their system, an event which causes it to "snap" (as Martha puts it in one extraordinary scene) and which leaves both partners terrified of the loss of this mutual attachment object and the intimacy implied by exposing and, thus, removing it from between them.

After continual drinking and intermittent bitter arguing, George and Martha insist on driving Nick and Honey home. Honey, quite

---

inebriated by this time, insists they stop at a roadside bar to dance. This interlude turns into a brawl in which Martha ridicules George further and which ends with George trying to strangle her. George initiates a game of "Get the Guests," breaking Nick's confidence by revealing a secret that Nick has confided to him: that he married Honey in response to a pseudocyesis (false pregnancy). Nick and Honey, hurt and furious, leave to walk home. George and Martha remain in the club parking lot where they continue to fight, finally declaring "total war."

Leaving George to walk home, Martha drives away, picks up Nick and Honey along the road, takes them back to the house, leaves Honey passed out in the back seat of the car, and takes Nick upstairs to seduce him. George arrives to catch a glimpse of them making love through the bedroom window. This ignites his despair and rage, and, determined to get back at Martha, he decides to "kill off' the imaginary son that has kept their relationship intact. George wanders off into the night, while Honey staggers into the house and sequesters herself in the bathroom. After coming downstairs, Martha wanders outside looking for George. Soon Martha and Nick reenter the house and Martha mockingly denigrates Nick's sexual performance and demotes him to the status of "houseboy." George soon enters, bearing a bouquet of snapdragons he's picked from the garden.

> *GEORGE (*Affecting embarrassment*) I . . . I brungya dese flowers, Mart'a, 'cause I . . . wull, 'cause you'se . . . awwwww hell. Gee.
>
> MARTHA: Pansies! Rosemary! Violence! My wedding bouquet!
>
> NICK (*Starting to move away*): Well, if you two kids don't mind, I think I'll just. . . .
>
> MARTHA: Ach! You just stay where you are. Make my hubby a drink.
>
> NICK: I don't think I will.
>
> GEORGE: No, Martha, no; that would be too much; he's your houseboy, baby, not mine.
>
> NICK: I'm nobody's houseboy. . . .
>
> GEORGE *and* MARTHA: . . . Now! (*Sing*) I'm nobody's house-

---

boy now . . . (*Both laugh*)
NICK: Vicious. . . .
GEORGE (*Finishing it for him*) . . . children. Hunh? That's right? Vicious children, with their oh-so-sad games, hopscotching their way through life, etcetera, etcetera. Is that it?
NICK: Something like it.
GEORGE: Screw, baby.
MARTHA: Him can't. Him too fulla booze.
GEORGE: Weally? (*Handling the snapdragons to* Nick) Here; dump these in some gin. Nick *takes them, looks at them, drops them on the floor at his feet*)
MARTHA (*Sham dismay*): Awwwwwww.
GEORGE: What a terrible thing to do . . . to Martha's snapdragons.
MARTHA: Is that what they are?
GEORGE: Yup. And here I went out into the moonlight to pick 'em for Martha tonight, and for our sonny-boy tomorrow, for his birfday (pp. 196-197).

George and Martha's victimizing teamwork begins to feel too close, too intimate, and they retreat to arguing once again. Honey soon reappears, and it becomes clear that Nick's disclosure of the reason for their marriage has caused a major breach of trust in their relationship. George, still stung by Martha's infidelity, announces that while she was upstairs with Nick a telegram arrived with the message that their "son" had been "killed" in an automobile accident. Martha fights off this news, becoming more and more frantic and begging George to stop taunting her with this cruel game. But, undaunted, George proceeds, and among the final scenes of the play is a symbolic funeral for the imaginary son (ironically, on his "birthday"), leaving both couples spent, bereft, and faced with the futility of the games, secrets, and myths that have cohered their partnerships.

*Early in the play, during one of her tirades, Martha recalls a joke at her father's party. To her great amusement, one of the guests had appropriated the tune, "Who's Afraid of the Big Bad Wolf?" and, in an effort at erudite sophistication, changed the words to "Who's Afraid of

Virginia Woolf?" At the play's end, George, now trying to comfort his grieving, emotionally depleted wife, sings, almost whispering: "Who's Afraid of Virginia Woolf, Virginia Woolf, Virginia Woolf. . . . Who's Afraid of Virginia Woolf . . ." Martha replies, abjectly, "I . . . am . . . George. . . . I . . . am. . . ." (p. 242).

IMPLICATIONS FOR CLINICAL PRACTICE

The protagonists in this play are, of dramatic necessity, drawn *in extremis.* But less extreme versions of the affects and behaviors displayed by George and Martha will be familiar to most therapists who see couples. Unwittingly, George and Martha have precipitated a crisis in their relationship. Couples like them often come for help when old balances have been upset and the previous relationship rules and roles no longer serve their function of fending off separation and/or intimacy anxiety. These relational crises are, paradoxically, junctures of great distress and potential opportunities for change. Alongside the despair that marks the end of "Who's Afraid of Virginia Woolf?" is a sense that, with their maladaptive defensive games stripped away, George and Martha have a chance to achieve a more desirable and mutually gratifying balance between intimacy and autonomy. We have the hope that they can learn to be "alone together."

How can clinicians help couples achieve this "separation that is not a separation but a form of union" (Winnicott, 1971a, p. 98)? First they must provide a holding environment or "potential space" for the couple that allows them to give voice to their anger, sorrow, fear, and other primary affects in a safe place. To build and sustain such an environment may require the clinician to survive intense exchanges with and between the partners without retaliating. While this posture implies understanding and acceptance of the couple's feelings, it also implies setting limits and boundaries on their destructiveness. In combining empathy with boundary setting, the clinician draws on a synthesis of behavioral, psychodynamic, and systemic strategies.

Feldman's (1979) approach effectively integrates these strategies. He suggests that the first step in intervention may be to help the couple learn to communicate non-aversively. This may require behavioral rehearsal, contingency contracting, role playing, and modeling. Simple exercises like assigning partners the task of not interrupting each other for short periods can help them build affect tolerance. Similarly, helping couples learn to use "I" statements is an effective tool for reducing projective identification as each partner is encouraged to "own" his or her own uncomfortable affects. Of course when substance abuse is an issue, as is the case with George and Martha, initial interventions may need to focus on modifying this behavior before undertaking other helping efforts.

Psychodynamic issues can be addressed as transference reactions toward the clinician arise and fears of intimacy find expression in such behaviors as lateness, missed appointments, or similar defensive tactics. Simultaneously, the clinician can tune into his or her own subjective responses to gather clues about what's going on with the couple and what's evolving in the therapeutic relationship. Feelings of helplessness, emptiness, sorrow, boredom, sexual arousal, or rage in the clinician often herald the appearance of similar but unexpressed feelings in the couple. The clinician's ability to "hold" these affects for partners until they can begin to experience and tolerate them more directly serves a crucial clinical function.

As they become more able to contain the range of strong feelings that close relationships evoke, partners can begin to recalibrate the couple system. Structural and strategic techniques such as sculpting and role-exchange exercises are helpful during this phase. Asking a couple to trade chairs and reverse roles in the dialogue, for example, can enhance empathy by temporarily altering typical patterns of interaction. Creatively integrated within an object relations framework, social learning, psychodynamic, and systemic approaches can help couples change the dynamics of their developmental dialectic toward more gratifying mutuality.

REFERENCES

Albee, E. (1983). *Who's afraid of Virginia Woolf?* New York: Penguin Putnam. (Original work published 1962).

Angyal, A. (1973). *Neurosis and treatment: A holistic theory.* New York: Viking.

Applegate, J. S. (1993). The developmental dialectic: Its place in clinical listening. *Clinical Social Work Journal, 21,* 125-135.

Bacal, H. A. (1990). John Bowlby. In H. A. Bacal & K. M. Newman (Eds.), *Theories of object relations: Bridges to self psychology* (pp. 207-222). New York: Columbia University Press.

Blanck, G., & Blanck, R. (1979). *Ego psychology II: Psychoanalytic developmental psychology.* New York: Columbia University Press.

Bowlby, J. (1977). The making and breaking of affectional bonds. *British Journal of Psychiatry, 130,* 201-210.

Bowlby, J. (1988). *A secure base: Parent-child attachment and healthy human development.* New York: Basic Books.

Feldman, L. B. (1979). Marital conflict and marital intimacy: An integrative psychodynamic-behavioral-systemic model. *Family Process, 18,* 69-78.

Freud, S. (1963). Analysis terminable and interminable. In P. Rieff (Ed.), *Therapy and technique: The collected papers of Sigmund Freud* (pp. 233-271). New York: Collier. (Original work published 1937).

Grotstein, J. S. (1989). Winnicott's importance in psychoanalysis. In M. G. Fromm & B. L. Smith (Eds.), *The facilitating environment: Clinical applications of Winnicott's theory* (pp. 130-158). Madison, CT: International Universities Press.

Klein, M. (1975). *Envy and gratitude and other works, 1946-1963.* New York: Delacorte.

Mahler, M. S., Pine, F., & Bergman, A. (1975). *The psychological birth of the human infant.* New York: Basic Books.

Ogden. T. H. (1990a). On potential space. In P. L. Giovacchini (Ed.), *Tactics and techniques in psychoanalytic therapy III: The implications of Winnicott's contributions* (pp. 90-112). Northvale, NJ: Jason Aronson.

Ogden, T. H. (1990b). *The matrix of the mind: Object relations and the psychoanalytic dialogue.* Northvale, NJ: Jason Aronson.

Shor, J., & Sanville, J. (1978). *Illusion in loving: A psychoanalytic approach to the evolution of intimacy and autonomy.* Los Angeles: Double Helix Press.

Sperling, M. B., & Berman, W. H. (Eds.) (1994). *Attachment in adults: Clinical and developmental perspectives.* New York: Guilford.

Stern, D. (1985). *The interpersonal world of the infant.* New York: Basic Books.

Winnicott, D. W. (1953). Transitional objects and transitional phenomena: A study of the first not-me possession. *International Journal of Psycho-Analysis, 34,* 89-97.

Winnicott, D. W. (1958). The capacity to be alone. In *The maturational processes and the facilitating environment* (pp. 29-36). Madison, CT: International Universities Press, 1965.

Winnicott, D. W. (1963). The development of a capacity for concern. In *The maturational processes and the facilitating environment* (pp. 73-82). Madison, CT: International Universities Press, 1965.

Winnicott, D. W. (1971a). The location of cultural experience. In *Playing and reality* (pp. 95-103). London: Tavistock.

Winnicott, D. W. (1971b). The place where we live. In *Playing and reality* (pp. 104-110). London: Tavistock.

Commitment: Implications for Couple Therapy

Marshall Jung

SUMMARY. This article addresses the issue of commitment and its importance in developing and sustaining an enriching relationship. The author describes commitment, its dynamics, and its implications for treating couples in conflict. The author also describes the conditions in which the issue of commitment is addressed in therapy and treatment interventions that can be used to help couples resolve their differences. *[Article copies available for a fee from The Haworth Document Delivery Service: 1-800-342-9678. E-mail address: <getinfo@haworthpressinc.com> Website: <http://www.HaworthPress.com>]*

KEYWORDS. Commitment, marital therapy, marriage, family therapy, commitment issues

Susan and Jim, living together but not married for nearly two years, came to me for therapy. They were a "reactive" couple, acting and reacting to the other's thoughts and feelings. They were unable to resolve the slightest differences of opinion. Their major problem centered on commitment, a common but seldom explored concern in the literature on couple therapy. Susan wanted to be married, while Jim was ambivalent. He repeatedly tried to convince her of his love and

---

Marshall Jung, DSW, is Professor of Social Work, Department of Social Work, California State University, San Bernardino, 5500 University Parkway, San Bernardino, CA 92407-2397.

[Haworth co-indexing entry note]: "Commitment: Implications for Couple Therapy." Jung, Marshall. Co-published simultaneously in *Journal of Couples Therapy* (The Haworth Press, Inc.) Vol. 9, No. 1/2, 2000, pp. 127-144; and: *Couples Connecting: Prerequisites of Intimacy* (ed: Barbara Jo Brothers) The Haworth Press, Inc., 2000, pp. 127-144. Single or multiple copies of this article are available for a fee from The Haworth Document Delivery Service [1-800-342-9678, 9:00 a.m. - 5:00 p.m. (EST). E-mail address: getinfo@haworthpressinc.com].

devotion and of his remaining in the relationship. For Jim, marriage was "just a piece of paper" and was not required for developing and maintaining a loving partnership. Susan, however, felt she was "walking on quicksand," and that, unless married, there were no assurances in the relationship. The couple was at the point of separating, Susan giving an ultimatum that unless they were married, she would leave.

This article examines the issue of marital commitment, henceforth referred to simply as *commitment*. More specifically, the author describes the meaning and dynamics of commitment, as well as its psychological and interpersonal implications. The author also describes general treatment considerations when addressing commitment issues. In addition, circumstances under which problems regarding commitment are brought to treatment and alternatives for addressing them are discussed. Vignettes from cases are used to illustrate concepts, principles of practice and techniques presented.

THE MEANING OF COMMITMENT

Many people believe love is a "decision," but falling in love is a mystery, something that happens to us, rather than something we choose. I have worked with many spouses who eventually asked for a divorce because they could not make themselves choose to love their partners, even though they genuinely liked and cared about them. However, we must be open to a loving relationship in order to develop one.

Although love and commitment influence one another, they are independent variables. There are, for example, many relationships in which individuals experience mutual love, but there is no commitment for marriage. Conversely, there are many relationships in which there is the absence of mutual love, but partners are committed to their marriages.

In enriching marriages, a commitment is a pledge or promise or vow freely given which binds individuals together on a path in life that is founded on hope and love, trust, friendship and respect. That pledge, which couples ordinarily believe will be binding forever, becomes legal, and for some solemn, when individuals exchange marital vows. A vow is extremely important because it is one's word and the basis for integrity. In the exchange of vows, partners articulate the promises on which the foundation of the marriage will be based.

Although the words or phrases may vary, the essence of most marital vows is that the partners will love, cherish, honor, support, and nurture each other. Implicit in the speaking of the words is that the relationship will be based on the oaths exchanged and that the partners will do all they can to foster a successful marriage.

Intricately involved in making a commitment is a person's very existence and purpose in life. Who someone is and who one will become, is influenced by the chosen partner more than anyone else. As indicated in Figure I, relationships are layered, and the further away from the center one goes, the less influence individuals will generally have on self perceptions, behaviors, and decision-making. The inner ring reflects the interdependency that is established and the loving union couples seek when they marry. When individuals marry, they each move from an "I" to a "we" position in relating to the world.

FIGURE I. Layers of Relationships

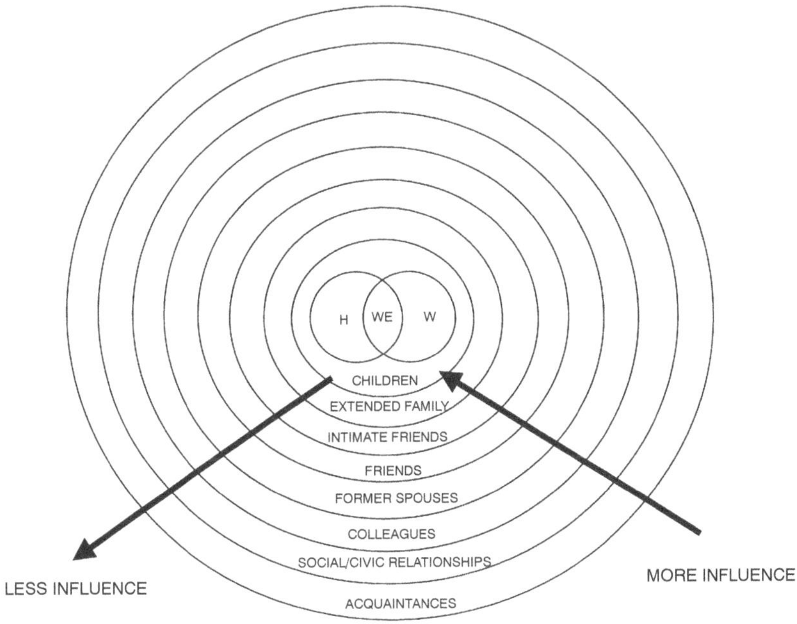

Consequently, in making a commitment, each "surrenders" oneself to being vulnerable to and influenced by the partner. Where each one goes, what each one does, what each one plans to do in the future, even how each feels and perceives oneself will be influenced by the partner or spouse more than anyone else. That influence can be a positive one in which there is mutual growth and enhancement, intimacy, and a deeper discovery and manifestation of oneself in the world, or it can be a negative one in which we stifle or block personal growth, feel resentful, and lose ourselves in the relationship by thinking, behaving, and feeling in a manner that is contrary to what each believes about his or her own self. Thus, the decision to make or not make a commitment to marry or remain in a marriage is a crucial one because so much is at stake.

There is no guarantee or assurance that any marriage will evolve into a mutually enhancing and satisfying relationship. Consequently, the feeling of hopefulness is also intricately involved in making a commitment. In marriage, each partner looks hopefully to the future based on love and trust to fulfill what was explicated in the marital vows. To develop and sustain a hopeful relationship, mutual respect, emotional support, and fulfilling one another's needs is required. The last dynamic to go in an unhappy marriage is hope, and the opposite of hope is despair. I have worked with many couples who no longer loved or trusted their partner, but were still hopeful things could improve. It was only after they. had given up hope that they felt they could proceed with a divorce.

If the foundation for an enriching marriage is based on hopefulness, the commitment to the relationship should be predicated upon freedom, that is, freedom to choose whom to marry based on love for its own sake. Furthermore, successful marriages require spouses to freely relinquish certain liberties, modify behaviors, and take into consideration their partner's thoughts and feelings in making decisions. Individuals are willing to do so because in return they are provided with the opportunity to demonstrate trust, respect, and love. However, freely committing to a marriage does not mean giving up autonomy or freedom to grow personally. In fact, it is the opposite. Freedom allows for personal growth. Thus, at a deeper level, partners give up nothing, but instead move ahead in life on a more enriching path.

On the other hand, if partners commit to a marriage out of fear, guilt, coercion, insecurity, or obligation, they have put themselves and their partners into an emotional prison. Such relationships are based on dependency and expectations rather than autonomy and hopefulness. Furthermore, once the immediate needs for marrying are met, they are burdened with and trapped into trying to fulfill the obligations and responsibilities of a marriage. This often leads to feelings of frustration, anger, resentment, and a circular pattern of interacting that is based on conflict, rigidity, and control. Thus, the foundation of such marriages is based on loss of freedom and personal growth, with each partner expecting the other to meet their needs. In such marriages, spouses tend to lose sight of, rather than discover, more about themselves.

The fact that so much is at risk when we marry has led me to believe that a judgment needs to precede the decision to marry. A judgment goes much deeper than a decision. A decision involves using problem-solving skills to examine daily issues, related to the advantages and disadvantages of the choices before me, such as whether or not to buy a used or new car, where to go on vacation, or what to purchase for holiday gifts. A judgment, on the other hand, addresses internal issues having to do with the self, personal integrity, and the future. A judgement involves knowing oneself and discerning the truth as to whether or not who someone is and someone wishes to be can be expressed and affirmed in the relationship. It also involves whether or not the opportunity for personal growth and development can continue and be reflected in the various aspects of the marriage. This includes having and raising children, involvement with extended family members, the direction of career and aspirations, the selection of friends, and the practicing of religion. Finally, a judgment involves knowing the partner and whether or not one is the person who can encourage him or her to be the person he or she wishes to become. In couple therapy, my work often focuses on helping clients make a judgment regarding these issues.

RAMIFICATIONS OF A COMMITMENT

The ramifications of making a commitment are illustrated in Figure II. The Figure portrays the outgrowths of commitment as being interrelated and fluid with no clear demarcations. Although the impact of a commitment on a couple is more than the sum of the variables involved, for analysis and discussion the elements are presented separately. The

FIGURE II. Dynamics of Commitment

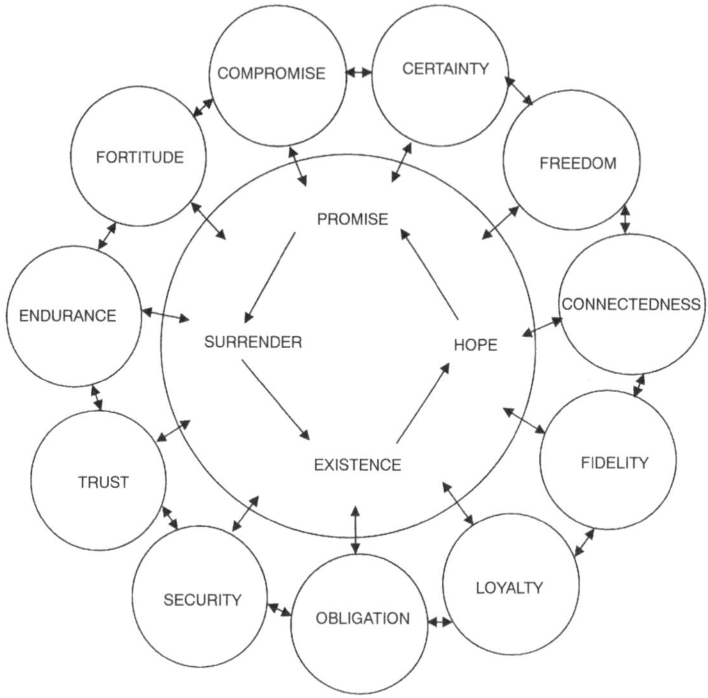

inner circle represents the individual's existence, promises made, hope, and ability to surrender. The smaller circles describe what can be hoped for as a result of a commitment: (1) certainty; (2) connectedness; (3) fidelity; (4) loyalty; (5) obligation; (6) security; (7) trust; (8) endurance; (9) fortitude; and (10) compromise.

Certainty

Couples must experience a reasonable amount of certainty that each partner desires to be together the remainder of his or her life. This certainty will include the willingness to engage and resolve or overcome the many misunderstandings, problems, changes, and adversities that all relationships must face. The commitment and the belief regarding the partner's willingness to invest in the partnership helps provide that certainty. This does not equate to a guarantee that loved ones will be available to one another at all times because that is impossible. This does not guarantee that my partner will forever remain in the relationship because no one can foretell the future. We can only hope that the promises given will be fulfilled. However, certainty does provide sufficient trust between the couple that the relationship can continue to move forward in a positive direction.

Connectedness

Knowing that my partner has freely committed himself or herself to me facilitates a connectedness that is based upon trust, respect, and friendship. This connection expresses itself in nurturing, intimacy, and self-sacrifice. It also allows each partner to know that the other is present emotionally, and for some, spiritually. Finally, with such connectedness, the fundamental human need for a loving companionship is met.

Fidelity

In most Western wedding ceremonies, couples pledge their fidelity, making it explicit that as part of their commitment the relationship will be an exclusive one. Remaining faithful to that promise is an affirmation of love and a sign of integrity, devotion to the partner, and honoring of the commitment. Furthermore, only with such a stipulation can an intimate relationship be developed and sustained. In addition to the loving feelings experienced, being bound together in such a manner helps to promote trust, friendship, and respect.

Loyalty

Issues of loyalty are often raised in couple therapy with spouses believing their partners are more loyal to others, such as their families of origin, children or stepchildren, or friendships. Implicit in making a commitment is the belief that each partner's loyalty and allegiance to the other will demonstrate protection, fidelity, devotion, support, and dependability, particularly under adverse conditions. Such loyalty promotes feelings of safety and cohesiveness, which are vital attributes of marriage. Without loyalty, couples feel their relationship is fragmented and in the process of disintegration.

Obligation

A commitment binds us to innumerable obligations or responsibilities, many of which are not easily undertaken or enjoyed. They are, however, necessary for maintaining a peaceful and smooth running home, providing mutual support, and developing personal growth. Responsibilities include sharing in household duties and child rearing, being encouraging of each other's career plans, and taking into consideration the partner's beliefs and feelings when decisions are being considered.

Security

When a commitment is based on love and freedom, a warm connectedness, fidelity, loyalty, and the fulfillment of obligations, couples feel a deep sense of security that the relationship will continue to grow in a positive manner. Such security allows partners to recognize they are loved for themselves as it fosters loving feelings and promotes trust.

Trust

Love cannot be proved but only demonstrated through actions. Trust provides the foundation upon which that demonstration can be accepted positively. I have worked with many couples who cannot, or will not, accept their partner's loving gestures, because they do not trust them. This is particularly true following a long history of unresolved conflicts and misunderstandings or devastating experiences such as an affair or physical violence.

Commitment is the first major step towards developing profound trust. Such trust is deeper than simply believing that one's partner will remain faithful, fulfill obligations, or provide encouragement. The deeper the trust, the more partners can be themselves with each other. Furthermore, the deeper the trust, the deeper the level of intimacy experienced. At the deepest level, there is no ego involvement with partners being available and completely present to each other.

Endurance

All relationships must encounter, tolerate, and overcome misunderstandings, pain, and adversity if an intimate relationship is to be achieved. A commitment acknowledges the willingness of spouses to endure hardships so that eventually conflicting issues, insecurities, and betrayals can be resolved, dissolved, or healed. I am constantly amazed by the level of endurance, emotional sacrifice and forgiveness clients have demonstrated because of their love and commitment. I recall, for example, a recent case in which the wife waited for several months in emotional turmoil while her husband decided whether or not he would remain in the marriage or continue to pursue another relationship. He, too, was in emotional turmoil, feeling guilty about his extramarital affair and the impact a divorce would have on his wife, children, and family.

Fortitude

A commitment fosters the belief and attitude that any problem or issue in the relationship can successfully be negotiated and resolved. Such confidence is self-perpetuating, and a profound sense of fortitude is internalized. Building on successes, couples believe they have the courage, patience, and the support of one another to face and overcome any problems the future may hold.

Compromise

Compromises or concessions must be made by spouses to negotiate successfully and overcome the innumerable differences and adversities that are a part of any marriage. The ability to compromise, a life-long process, requires empathy, flexibility, and good communication and problem-solving skills. If couples continue to find success in their ability to compromise, it evolves into an art, with partners using their imagination and creativity to find solutions for the most complex and difficult issues.

GENERAL TREATMENT ISSUES

There is no formula to helping couples address the issue of commitment. Although there may be many similarities between couples, each has a unique developmental history and distinct set of circumstances that have led them to seek therapy. We must, therefore, work collaboratively with them to clarify their problems and develop a special treatment plan that helps to meet their particular needs. To accomplish these tasks, the following therapeutic processes are recommended.

Helping Couples to Clearly Define Issues

It has been my experience that for couples who are not married, like Susan and Jim mentioned above, the problems that have brought them to treatment are clearly seen as being related to the issue of commitment. However, for married couples, the matter of commitment is often not recognized as being the central problem. Instead, conflicts are organized around whether or not one or both spouses wish to remain in the relationship or are willing to put effort into improving the relationship. In such circumstances, I help clients to "reframe" their concerns so they may understand their fundamental problems with commitment.

For many couples, the inability to recognize the problem as being associated with commitment is hindered by feelings of resentment and/or inability to communicate effectively. Both resentment and poor communication obstruct the ability to perceive rationally and objectively. Consequently, the initial intervention for many couples is to assist them in resolving these two issues.

Other couples begin treatment with various presenting problems such as domestic violence, substance abuse, or irreconcilable differences. Through the process of treatment, they discover their problems go deeper and that they are disillusioned with the marriage. As a result, they question whether or not they can overcome mistrust, recapture friendship, or retrieve the respect or loving feelings they once held for the other. In therapy, I will lead the couple to a discussion on the issue of commitment.

Helping Couples to Understand the Dynamics of Commitment

Many couples have difficulty comprehending the dynamics of commitment. Using the illustration in Figure II, I help such couples gain a clearer understanding of its meaning. For married couples, this includes helping them recognize that the basis for a marriage can vary and that many couples decide to remain together for a variety of reasons other than mutual love. These reasons include concern for the well being of the partner, obligation to their children, extended family, and/or religious or cultural beliefs. We then discuss the importance of being clear regarding the type of commitment on which a marriage is based.

Helping Couples Select a Treatment Plan

There is no formula to helping couples address the issue of commitment. Therapists must be flexible, creative, and adaptive to the particular circumstances and needs of their clients. Some couples will need to be seen conjointly, others, concurrently, or combined conjointly and concurrently. Some couples will require or prefer a communication, problem solving, or task-centered approach while others require a solution-focused, affective, or reflective method of treatment. For many, a structured separation is necessary for helping judge whether or not they wish to remain in their marriage. With such couples, the use of Jung's (1998) "Application of Individuation Therapy to Structured Separations" may be very helpful.

No matter which approach or method I use to assist my clients, I require that between sessions they commit to working on the issues addressed in treatment two times for at least one hour. Clients are normally very receptive to this requirement because they recognize how it empowers them, fosters movement, and maximizes the benefits that can be derived from treatment. Clients actively participate in formulating the tasks and in the discussion regarding benefits or outcomes that can be derived from them.

Defining the Therapist Role in the Therapeutic Process

In the initial session, I ask couples what they expect of me. They often have unrealistic expectations. They perceive me as someone who will tell them what to do, and/or act as a judge. I correct these and other misconceptions. I then share that I must maintain neutrality while using my body of knowledge and skills to provide information and useful insights. I also share with them that therapy is a collaborative process which involves us working together to devise a treatment plan that will meet their unique needs. Finally, I share with them that I will need to adapt to their particular circumstances, and therefore, my role during treatment may change. At times I may act as a reflective listener, mediator, or consultant while at other times as an educator, resource person, or broker.

Fostering and Maintaining the Therapeutic Process

Once the therapeutic plan has been devised, my task is to assist clients in implementing it. In addition, I must monitor the plan to determine its effectiveness and, if necessary, to work with my clients to change it altogether if it is not meeting the required objectives. To help foster a safe and helpful therapeutic process, I must work to keep couples present and future oriented, diffuse emotional blocks, prevent negative circular patterns of communication or behavior in the session, and ensure that both parties participate actively in the therapeutic process.

CIRCUMSTANCES IN WHICH ISSUES REGARDING COMMITMENT ARE BROUGHT TO TREATMENT

This section describes the circumstances in which the issue of commitment is addressed in treatment. Case examples will be used to illustrate particular problems and treatment interventions.

Fear of Making a Commitment–Not Living Together

The building of a loving relationship is an evolutionary and developmental process. Normally it begins with attraction and then proceeds on to dating, "falling in love" in which the relationship becomes exclusive, and then engagement when a commitment to marry has been made. Many individuals, however, feel or believe they cannot do the latter. Some question whether or not they love their partner while others, having been divorced, do not wish to risk marriage again but want the relationship to continue. Many have other reasons why they do not wish to marry their partner, but they also wish the relationship to continue. However, there are a few, like my former client Saul, who never fully understood why he had to end his long turn relationship with Kristin.

Saul came to me unable to make a commitment to Kristin, a loving and intimate friend for two years. Initially, we focused on examining the strengths and weakness of the relationship, addressing and resolving deep insecurities regarding his self-worth. We also focused on what happened in former relationships and on resolving family of origin issues. By the end of treatment, Saul felt centered and was at peace with himself. Concerning the issue which initially brought him to me, Saul decided to end the relationship with Kristin. He could not, however, articulate any "reasonable" explanation as to his decision. He simply "knew" that who he was and who he wanted to become could not be fulfilled with her.

Fear of Making a Commitment–Living Together

There are several reasons why couples elect to live together without marrying. Some, for example, do it for companionship and support without any expectations for a commitment while others use living together as a "trial" marriage to determine whether or not they are compatible. In any case, relationships become complex when individuals live together. Issues of compatibility, loyalty, responsibility, obligation, and decision-making have to be negotiated satisfactorily if a peaceful coexistence is to exist. In many respects the relationship takes on many aspects of a marriage with the couple establishing a "we psyche" or emotional state of inter-connectedness. The bond of inter-connectedness, whether positive or negative, is intensified and deepened as the relationship progresses. Couples become interdependent both physically and emotionally, with each turning to the other to meet their physical and emotional needs.

Gary, age twenty-three and Susan, age 25, were seen in couple treatment after having lived together for a little over three years. The issue of commitment was never raised until Susan decided she wanted to be married and have children. Gary immediately balked at the idea stating that he was "too young" to have children. The couple sought my help because they were continually arguing over the issue. They felt they had reached an impasse with Susan demanding that Gary either marry her or end the relationship. Following the initial session, I saw the couple in "concurrent individuation" therapy described by Jung (1993). The decision to see them separately was based on the fact that Gary felt restricted in being able to share with me his thoughts and feelings in front of Susan.

During my initial session with Gary he revealed that his problem with marrying went deeper than not wishing to have children. Susan's wish for marriage awoke in him the belief that he had not sufficiently dated and that although he loved her, he wanted to end the relationship so he could meet other women. However, he could not tell her the truth because he felt guilty for not giving her what she wanted. He also was afraid of hurting her feelings, knowing that ending the relationship would cause her tremendous despair.

I first used affective interventions to help Gary clarify his feelings. He concluded he was not feeling guilty because he had broken a morale code and not been honest with Susan regarding their relationship. However, he also concluded he would be responsible for hurting Susan if he proceeded with a separation. Addressing this issue, I used reality therapy intervention by indicating to him that he was faced with a dilemma, meaning no matter what decision he made regarding the relationship, one of the two was going to be hurt. If he remained in the relationship, he would be miserable and if he ended it, she would feel devastated. After a great deal of reflection and exploration, Gary recognized that if he remained in the relationship both, in fact, would be unhappy because he would feel trapped in the relationship. Following this insight, he proceeded to tell Susan about his desire to date.

Opposition of Children Regarding Their Parents Remarrying

In a few instances, I have worked with couples where one parent's children were adamantly opposed to their remarrying. Reasons for their opposition included loyalty to their natural parent, dislike of their parent's partner, and feelings of jealousy regarding sharing the attention and affection of the parent's with another. When these issues were presented, I used a problem solving approach to assist parents in trying to rectify their children's concerns. When this was not possible, I continued with the same treatment approach to help the couple make a decision regarding the relationship. Some couples chose to end their relationship, while others decided to remain together but not marry until the children left home.

In some families, the opposition to parents marrying is a manifestation of other problems between parents and their children. In these circumstances, I use structural family therapy to address the issues presented.

Intrusion of Parents

There are times when parents object to their children marrying a certain person. This is often a reflection of unresolved family of origin issues, in which case I use structural family therapy to assist clients.

However, there are instances when the issue is related to cultural and/or religious differences between parents and their children. I have, for example, worked with Chinese clients whose parents opposed their marriage because they were marrying a non-Chinese. In such cases I frame the problem as a "cultural dilemma." To address this dilemma, I share with the client that I believe he/she will need to make a "judgment" regarding the importance of marrying against their parents' wishes and the implication of that decision on "who they are and what they value." I also share my belief that upon making the judgment, he/she will integrate what they believe to be good from both American and Chinese culture and thereby find inner peace.

To help clients make a judgment, I request they set time aside between sessions to "reflect" on the issues before them. I suggest three one-half hour periods during the week in which they sit alone and undisturbed. I then explain to them Carl Jung's process of "active imagination," and how it can be used to help resolve their dilemma. I then coach them in its use.

Irreconcilable Differences

There are situations where I treat couples with irreconcilable differences. I recall, for example, when one partner insisted that their children be raised Catholic. His Jewish fiancee would not consent to the demand. I used a problem solving approach with this couple and other couples who place a condition on committing to marrying. If couples decide they must discontinue the relationship, I use a separation therapy to help them end the relationship in a manner that is least damaging and painful to those involved. Sometimes this includes children, friends and prospective in-laws.

Ambivalence Regarding Remaining in the Marriage

Some couples seek therapy after they have reached the "disillusionment" stage of divorce. In this stage, the integrity of the relationship is threatened because spouses question whether or not they wish to remain committed to it. With such couples, I generally begin with a problem-solving approach to help couples address the issues regarding their ambivalence. In many instances, however, couples remain ambivalent. Reasons for remaining doubtful include strong feelings of resentment, spouses feeling "trapped" in the relationship, and secret extramarital affairs.

When I am not able to work conjointly with couples to resolve their ambivalence about continuing the relationship, I suggest to them a trial separation. In doing so, I explain to them how a separation can be used to help rectify their situation.

Polarized Couples

Working with polarized couples can be extremely difficult because partners are coming to treatment with different objectives. One wants you to help keep the relationship together while the other wants to end it. If you support either one's position, the other generally does not return.

If I am not able to help couples come to an agreement on treatment objectives, I suggest concurrent rather than conjoint therapy. For clients wishing to remain in the marriage, the focus is on examining why they wish to remain in a relationship and what they might do to persuade their partner to change. For clients wishing to end the relationship, the focus is on examining the possibility for reconciliation and on what prevents them from leaving. With the latter, treatment often centers on helping resolve those issues. I recall for example, a client who believed if she left her husband, she would be ostracized by her minister and members of her congregation. She was encouraged to speak with them and after having done so, found them to be very supportive. She then proceeded with the separation by filing divorce papers.

Extramarital Affairs

Many spouses become ambivalent about remaining in their marriages because of an involvement in an extramarital affair. Those involved in an extramarital affair often find themselves feeling confused and overwhelmed. For example, some believe they "love their partner," but are no longer "in love" with him/her and therefore question whether or not they should they remain in their marriage. Others believe their lover meets all their unsatisfied needs, but feel guilty about proceeding with a divorce because of the hurt it would cause their children or because it is contrary to their religious beliefs.

In any case, I recommend to the person having the extramarital affair that they put the extramarital affair on hold until deciding whether or not to remain in the marriage. I go on to explain the reasons for my recommendation and then suggest concurrent individuation therapy. Separate treatment objectives are established in the individual sessions. I will proceed with either conjoint marital therapy or divorce therapy depending on whether or not the ambivalent partner decided to remain in the marriage.

CONCLUSION

The significance of a commitment is not based primarily upon a legal agreement that binds us together under the law. Instead, its importance is based upon the giving of our word that translates into the surrendering of oneself to the influence of the partner. When marital vows are exchanged, words bind partners together and provide a foundation upon which a mutually fulfilling partnership can be founded. For many, without a commitment, their relationship has no direction, and therefore, trust cannot be established. Intrinsically involved in making a commitment is hopefulness because there are no guarantees regarding what the future holds. Finally, couple therapy often involves helping clients make a judgment regarding whether or not they wish to commit or recommit to their relationship or marriage.

There are many dynamics associated with making a commitment. These dynamics help provide the foundation on which couples build their relationship. Consequently, the more understanding they have of these dynamics, the more likely they will successfully develop a sustaining loving partnership.

In many respects, the therapeutic process for working with the issue of commitment is similar to any other problem brought to treatment. The therapist needs to assist clients in defining their problems clearly, work collaboratively in establishing treatment objectives, and implementing, monitoring, evaluating, and if necessary, changing the treatment plan. In addition, however, therapists often need to help clients recognize that their problems center around the issue of commitment and what a commitment actually means.

The final section of this paper described eight conditions in which the issue of commitment is addressed in therapy. The issues presented were divided into two categories: deciding whether or not to marry and deciding whether or not to remain in the marriage. Treatment interventions were suggested, but readers are reminded that each case is unique and that they must adapt interventions that fit the particular circumstances of the couples with whom they are working.

REFERENCES

Jung, M. (1993). *Constructual marital therapy: Theory and practice.* New York: Gardner Press.

Jung, M. (1998). The implementation of individuation therapy with structured separations. *Journal of Couples Therapy, 7*, 69-85.

Index

For Product Safety Concerns and Information please contact our EU representative GPSR@taylorandfrancis.com Taylor & Francis Verlag GmbH, Kaufingerstraße 24, 80331 München, Germany